4

PUKKA INDIAN

© Roli Books, 2017
Second impression, 2018
© Text and Photographs Jahnvi Lakhota Nandan,
Shivani Gupta

Published in India by Roli Books
M-75, Greater Kailash II Market
New Delhi-110 048, India
Ph: ++91-11-40682000
E-mail: info@rolibooks.com
Website: www.rolibooks.com

ISBN: 978-93-5194-140-8

Printed and bound at
Nutech Print Services, India,

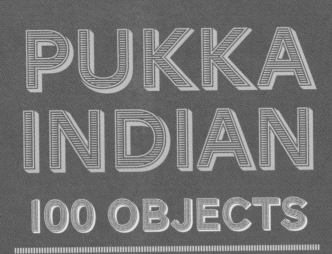

PUKKA INDIAN
100 OBJECTS
THAT DEFINE INDIA

JAHNVI LAKȞÓTA NANDAN

Lustre Press
Roli Books

CONTENTS

INTRODUCTION

DNA is the basis of life. It is what makes each of us unique. Design is the DNA of society and unique to every culture. The more we learn about the structure of a society's DNA, the more we see that design is the motor of life in every society. At the same time, design is also what distinguishes one group of people, one society, from another.

This book started with the intention to document the design of everyday objects: water pots and earthen cups, dishes, cars, clothes and all the things that make these objects relevant in daily Indian life. In the process of writing I discovered that to understand these objects one had to re-imagine design itself – what it means, what role it plays in people's lives and how its user influences the design of the product.

Design is a mirror of our attitudes and habits. Through the course of writing this book on Indian design, I found that uniquely Indian gestures like churning, combing and calculating were reflected in it. Objects used every day, like the bangles/bindi, pressure cooker, sari blouse, dupatta, tandoor, etc., all put a long tradition of design of household objects at the core of everyday life in the country. While other products like the Kalnirnay calendar, bahi-khata for bookkeeping, mandira, a tool used to churn milk into butter, all reflected these uniquely Indian habits.

Often the choice of material in Indian design is based on abundant availability and its relative affordability. Everyone has seen or sat on the tubular Godrej chairs, in fact now they are a collectors' favourite. Godrej started making these CH-4 chairs in the 1950s because steel was subsidized by the Indian government to encourage manufacturing. This same material has helped keep traditional objects such as utensils or 'bartans' current in every Indian household. In fact it also remains the material of choice for designers of the company Inox or for Driade that produced designer Maan Singh's Kachnar Bowls as they take designing with this material to newer heights.

Take organic materials such as cow dung cakes. Typically cow dung as a material for hand-crafted design would be considered with a certain amount of caution, if not outright disbelief, but not in India, where the multiple facets of cow dung usage reads as an anthology of ingenuity finding its way into fuel, construction as well as contemporary art. The importance given to the material shows that the act of making is as important as the product itself.

At my alma mater, the School of Art and Design at Tsukuba University, Japan, I realized that few contemporary cultures have as close a relationship with objects that were designed 7000 years ago as India does. Kitchen tools like the tava, the oldest of utensils in India used for centuries to roast the country's staple diet, are a testament to this long and uninterrupted use of objects. On a personal note, design also became the chain linking the

Famous as the world's cheapest car, the forward-thinking Nano embraces the consumer psyche of frugality as it aims to become the mainstay of urban driving.

last two decades of my life – the chain that propelled me to this architecture school and that brought me to Paris to design with the most elusive of all materials, smell, that in India finds expression through incense, soaps and attars.

The sheer number of noteworthy objects makes choosing what to include and what not to in a book like this extraordinarily complicated. So I chose to create a portrait of Indian design. The topic lit up many conversations. Everyone from friends to family offered suggestions that have helped make the list. The focus of these suggestions was often on 'Indian-ness', discussions around how the chess was definitely not of Indian origin or that there was nothing more Indian than the banta drink. But in the end, I decided that 'Indian-ness' was too vague a term, to create a portrait of design one had to go deeper.

Design has a complex relationship with origins. The Royal Enfield motorcycle, the Godrej Almirah and the pressure cooker were all 'foreign' but were re-drawn as products in India, giving them a new meaning. These products are a marriage of craft and industry and have given India a unique form characterized by appropriating something new and merging it with something old and something borrowed often referred to as 'jugaad'. Jugaad shows that India is intuitively adept at finding solutions through the oldest of human conditions – 'scarcity'. In time it became sophisticated as we see in the Nano where Indian design is at its most ingenious and adaptable. This product is a result of multiple constraints of cost, size and mobility. The Nano is small and frugal but has thirty-eight pending patents.
Designing with scarcity
is not a products-only

The LPG cylinder ushered in not only a change in cooking fuel but a redesign of the Indian kitchen for the first time in a few thousand years.

The humble tiffin distribution system proves that innovation and efficiency is inherent in grassroots mechanisms.

playground. 'Frugal' is a bit of a crude word, but has been adopted globally as an important design currency in an unpredictable world.

Scarcity implies simplicity of design. Draped clothes in their form are the most symbolic of this simplicity. Even at their most luxurious in the choice of materials, they maintain a purity of design. Draping remains the most loved expression for most contemporary fashion designers in India. The role of symbolism too has never been explored in design. But like the divine pair Shiva and Parvati, everything in Hindu cosmology has two sides – a symbolic and a material one. So I have included objects that are designed around symbols and markers of status, such as the bichiya and the mangalsutra. The flowers and conch shells of the bichiya are symbols of fertility. The ring is worn such that the pressure exerted on the toe helps relieve stress. The mangalsutra is one of the five identification marks of a married woman. Every mangalsutra is individualized but they all have black beads made of adobe. Adobe or clay from the earth is believed to be a protector and absorber of negative energies, and since the woman in a Hindu joint family was responsible for the peace and harmony of the family, it was essential

that she be protected from harmful disruptive energies. The expression of spirituality through belief systems like Ayurveda has led to the creation of many products that stem from traditional wisdom, like the neem datun used to clean teeth. But whereas wisdom in design is an expected feature, madness is an unexpected tour de force. In fact some products such as the chilli and lemon hanging from the door jamb or the dung cakes embody both.

I have included many tools from the Indian kitchen. These products evoke daily life at its most painterly and include the simple pleasures of everyday that are telling of an Indian attitude towards things. Utensils are a case in point. The first utensils were used for ritual purposes. Basins with a rim that resemble the patila came into existence in the proto-historic period. Fast forward centuries, water storage systems used today like the surahi or the matka are similar to the ones used for Vedic water rituals. The long-standing relationship stemming from their dual ritual and domestic use continues to inspire contemporary designers, in fact the Doshi Levien designed slip-cast version incorporates filtration, can be industrially produced, and is a greener alternative to bottled and refrigerated water.

The composition of perfumes has given me a privileged viewpoint of designing for and with the senses. It is in this sensory spirit of design that the Chyawanprash, the flower garland and the banta drink have been included. Like the paan, flower garlands too have always been one of the offerings to god. To design artefacts, clothes and jewellery for the gods involved using all the five senses – sound, colour, texture, smell and taste. Statues of gods are

*Proudly made of stainless steel, when launched, this almirah represented
modernity, today it continues to store the most precious of India's belongings.*

anointed with the colour and perfume that diffuses from the sandalwood and turmeric paste applied on them. Made further resplendent with garlands, these accessories stimulated the eyes, touch and the sense of smell, and are treated not just as decoration but also as objects with functions that appease all the five senses. Ordering of such seemingly disparate pieces of information as the senses constitutes design in its purest form.

One cannot forget that history too has had as much a sleight of hand in design as the designer. The independence movement that started in 1857 impacted the country's design and its economy through its fight for 'swadeshi'. Swadeshi was a nation-wide economic call aimed to boycott imported (British) products and opt for indigenously made ones. Such expressions of resistance and loyalty, where for every imported product an Indian product was created, gave rise to advertising and packaging design. Brands with a visually obvious Indian identity like Mysore Sandal Soap, Amrutanjan balm and Babuline gripe water were created. This defined the Indian consumer for generations after his or her quest for fair price and local production. This resistance has created 'icons' like the Nehru jacket.

With the choice of objects now made, I faced a whole new set of problems. For one thing, design-related documents for many of these products are non-existent. Nor is there a single 'creator' for most of them. So for each object I have set out to do two things. One, suggest the context of its creation and two, make a rough sketch, based on observation and deduction, of its design guidelines. Where these hundred objects truly reflect Indian design is in the fact that they are a combination of the straight lines of rationality, mathematics and weaving and the curved lines found in natural forms and the human body. The choice has never been for one or the other but

for both together. Coincidentally this combination is found in the script of most modern Indian writing systems such as Devanagari, a combination of curves aligned under straight lines. And like the script they have passed the ultimate test for design, that is, for society to accept it fully.

Society's response to a product is the most important measure of a design's calibre. Users inspire the product's creation and with time, if the product is successful, they become so emotionally connected with it that they take it for granted. This was my case and that of countless other people for whom the hundred objects chosen for this book of India's everyday design emerge as champions of design.

The precepts of Indian design are strong, carrying with them a romantic vision. Before long, history was helping actively to sustain the Indian design: think of Swadeshi, all the indigenous products it created are still used such as the Amrutanjan balm and Nehru jacket; think of the wisdom of the ancient combined with the wisdom of the visitors from distant lands, where the sil batta and the heavy grinder Sumeet mixer are used by the same hands – within a course of five minutes one has bridged thousands of years of design.

Now, even though some sophisticated industrial technology is available, the original Indian designs are preferred, like the Royal Enfield is still ridden by many on the streets of central Paris and the planter's chair graces Hollywood. Back home, the design, due to its continuous use, has become a firm belief of Indian society – and the country's image of itself. I couldn't help break into a smile when quite recently I heard a young global Indian traveller announce that it was impossible for her to leave the shores of the country without her kohlapuri chappals and her tongue cleaner.

100
OBJECTS
THAT DEFINE INDIA

In the words of Buckminster Fuller design can be described as 'the deliberate ordering of rather disparate components'. But actually the word design is not that easy to define – one has to look to its starting point to its materials, designers, forms, the model on which these forms are based, and also the intention that lies behind the creation of the product.

Shape and form, the most visible aspects of any given object of design, are of course of great importance in Indian design but this represents only one aspect of the whole. Matter or material is equally if not more important. This is an essential characteristic of Indian design. For material is derived from the word 'metre', a unit of measure, and the word 'measure' in the English language comes from the Sanskrit word 'maya', that has its root in mā, meaning 'to measure'.

AGARBATTI

Incense sticks are the oldest and purest form of perfume

Date of Origin: Before 700 CE
Material: Myrrh, costus, frankincense, agar wood and other natural and synthetic ingredients

Amongst all the senses, smell is perceived as transcendental, because it is invisible. So designing with smell poses many challenges. Incense offers a response to this. While solid and simple in shape, burning it releases a fragrant smoke. In fact even the word perfume means just that – 'through fumes'. Incense is therefore considered one of the ways to reach out to the divine. Amongst all the forms of perfumery, incense is the oldest and considered the purest. In India its daily lighting in all spaces is an unbroken tradition.

Offering of incense started during the Bhakti period in the seventh century as one of the five services to god. Natural ingredients like myrrh, costus, sandalwood, cardamom, patchouli, palmarosa, vetiver, rosha grass (Indian geranium), and lemongrass are pounded in a mortar and pestle or in a machine with water to make a paste. Flowers like roses and jasmine were introduced much later in the sixteenth century with the tradition of Indo-Persian perfumery. In contemporary India, synthetic ingredients like musks and aldehydes are added to give them a modern perfumistic quality. Adding saltpetre helps the material burn uniformly. This mix is then spread by hand around thin bamboo sticks and dried. While burning, heat releases the smell of the ingredients.

The earliest mention of incense has been in various medical texts as fumigation was believed to purify and protect. Over forty incense formulas are listed in the *Kasyapa Samhita*, a seventh-century medical text on child-birth and paediatrics. It refers to mainly two kinds of incense, the *dhupa* and the *pratidhupa*. Dhupa drives the demons away and pratidhupa is believed to bring in good fortune. Their therapeutic value was part of the know-how of the perfumer. For example, commonly used incense ingredients such as the resin myrrh, the widely found costus root and neem leaves have curative properties as powerful antiseptics.[1]

Incense had many other varied functions, such as to control elephants, repel insects or for sexual pleasure. Formulas changed depending on the purpose: to make incense for gods, the best resins had to be used, like costus; for the demons, heartwoods like aloes wood; for the enemies of gods, typical simple resins; and for humans, synthesized resins like sal resin or cane syrup.[2]

While the incense for gods was strict and came to be perceived as archaic, the incense for people was playful and open to experimentation, even to the exotic with ingredients like frankincense that were not common to India. But the startling fact is that all incense in India since the seventh century is made in a complex manner like modern twentieth-century French perfumes, with fumigations that had classifications such as principle, subsequent and after fumigations. In modern perfumery this is classified as top, middle and base notes. This tradition is what classifies Indian incense as unique and sets it apart from the rest of the world's incense traditions.

AMAR CHITRA KATHA

A comic series inspired from history and mythology

Date of Origin: 1967, Bombay, now Mumbai
Material: Paper

Until 1967, when Anant Pai created the first Amar Chitra Katha (ACK) comic, Indian mythology was usually transmitted orally. Grandparents told grandchildren bedtime stories of gods and goddesses. ACK comics gave relevance to this mythology by turning an oral tradition into comics. Thus, a centuries-old ritual became a product designed with strong visual elements.

Its creators combined an aesthetic borrowed from the calendar art style of Raja Ravi Varma and storytelling from cinema to produce illustrations. In the nineteenth century, Raja Ravi Verma, India's first lithographer started painting portraits that were to be distributed nationwide commercially as advertisements. India has diverse ethnicities, but he chose to paint one figure type that was a combination of different cultures from around the country; the body form was north Indian, the draping of the sari mostly Maharashtrian and the jewellery south Indian. His painting style was naturalistic and free-flowing, also a hallmark of the style that ACK adopted. This distinguished it from the other comics that were manga-like in the East or had more symbolic strength in the West. ACK's renderings were equally arty yet made for popular appreciation. They

became such a stylistic reference of Indian mythology that the popular television serials 'Mahabharata' and 'Ramayana' borrowed designs directly from them to make their sets look authentic. While most international comics feel more like reading a book, ACK felt like watching a film, with the storyline laid out in frames with animated close-ups of facial expressions. It is in this amalgamation of various styles that its originality exists.

But ACK is not only an amalgamation of different styles, it is also a unique mix of subject matter. Krishna was the first character, and the whole life of this demi-god offered a rich source of inspiration ranging from childish folly to divine wisdom. Characters like Ram and Sita from the epic *Ramayana* find equal mention with Akbar and Gandhi from history. Their stories have been illustrated alongside Batman, Mandrake and Dhyan Chand, the country's hockey legend. This hybrid of history, mythology, narrative and the secular is distinctly Indian and makes the ACK what it is: not just a comic book but the voice of a grandparent, the images of a history film and the frames of national portraits all rolled into one product designed for everybody's satisfaction.

AMRUTANJAN BALM

This balm, a favourite amongst freedom fighters, continues to be popular as a pain reliever

Date of Origin: 1893, Bombay
Material: Menthol, methyl salicylate and other ingredients

Ayurvedic texts prescribe the use of rose, camphor, eucalyptus and wintergreen for pain relief. These ingredients are to be combined into a paste and rubbed on the affected area. In 1893, an Ayurvedic doctor, Nageshwara Rao Panthulu patented a version of this Ayurvedic formulation and named it 'Amrutanjan', which means quite literally 'eternal life-giving ointment'. Heavily laced with large quantities of mint and wintergreen, it instantly became popular nationwide. Even today, its aromatic camphor-heavy fragrance, packaged in a mustard and green bottle, exemplifies the unique and unforgettable 'smell' of India.

Although an innocuous Ayurvedic product for healing headaches and muscle aches, Amrutanjan became an important symbol of swadeshi or Indian indigenous enterprise. Panthulu, the maker of Amrutanjan, himself was at the forefront of India's struggle for independence. In 1930, Mahatma Gandhi organized the salt march, a non-violent form of protest against taxes levied on Indian salt to promote a British monopoly. This was a twenty-three-day, four-hundred-kilometre march starting at the salt pans in west India. Panthulu was a part of this march and, in a clever marketing campaign, he freely handed out bottles of this mustard coloured balm to his fellow marchers. Panthulu was also the first Indian industrialist to use advertising.

The pain balm advertisement, one of the first examples of advertising in India, appeared on the front page of the Telugu newspaper *Andhrapatrika*, a newspaper of 'Andhra affairs' that began to be published out of Bombay in 1910. In the advertisement, a woman holding the balm appeared on the map of India. So far it had just been an innocuous Ayurvedic product for healing headaches and muscle aches, but the timing of this advertising was such that shortly after, the balm became one of the products that came to epitomize swadeshi.

After many years of soothing pain in history, the pain balm has moved from its swadeshi roots into a successful commercial realm. In 1936, it was listed on the Bombay Stock Exchange. With almost no change to its logo type or bottle or the yellow colour of the balm from its fragrant ingredients, it is still manufactured in Chennai. A new formulation with fewer ingredients, that is white in colour, hints at the competition from Vicks Vaporub and its likes. Amrutanjan balm stays current and popular as one of the three most preferred pain relievers in the country. But today's vector is neither a freedom fighter nor a soldier. It's a vibrant yellow, blue and green packaging, also sold in the shape of a roll-on deodorant stick, for stressed out headache-ridden compatriots in trains and offices.

ANGOOTHI
When jewellery embraces the divine

Date of Origin: Unknown
Material: Gold, silver, brass; precious and semi-precious stones

The choice of gemstones in the setting of jewellery in India is not based on aesthetics alone. Rings with coloured stones are worn by both men and women so that they can channel the energies of the stones to their benefit. There is a choice of nine stones, the major stones being diamonds, pearls, rubies and sapphires, and the minor ones could be chosen from a variety of different stones including the coral and topaz. The nine stones represent the *nava graha* that are the Sun, Mercury, Venus, Jupiter, Saturn, Moon, the ascending and descending nodes; not all, but only the Sun, Moon, Venus and Jupiter are considered lucky. The rest could be destructive and so their energies need to be controlled; this is done by the correct placement of these stones in a ring ensuring that the stone touches the skin. Setting stones in jewellery in India is born out of an understanding of a combination of astrology and astronomy and surpasses all jewellery-making techniques.

The basic design for the layout of the stones is either a square or a circle, two shapes that represent the absolute and infinity in Hinduism. The Hindu cosmology consists of deities representing the seven planets and the two moon cycles, with each of them having a representative colour of stone.[3] This collection set into a circle or a square is called the *navratna*, which represents the universe and the relationship of all its constituents. In unity, the nine stones are supposed to embody the power of the universe. The *navratna* rings are the most well-known articles of jewellery that are used for navratna stones, but in fact they can also be set into pendants, bangles, armlets, bracelets or various types of necklaces.

Like all agrarian cultures, Hindus revere the sun as the source of all life, its fire represented by the ruby – this stone is also the most significant amongst the nine stones and perhaps the most important one in the country. The sun diffuses white light when passed through a prism and it breaks down into seven colours, and hence the seven gemstones with two representing the nodes, thus nine in all, is the most auspicious number in Hindu astrology. The defence and cure provided by these seven stones is all about the right timing. The right timing to set each of the stones in the *navratna* jewellery and the right time to wear it constitute important astrological knowledge.[4] At its most precise potency it could take up to a year to set. In fact this astrological significance is not limited to the Hindus anymore but is shared by all religions of the subcontinent. Since Indians wearing *navratna* favour astrology over the preciousness of jewellery, interestingly more affordable stones like rubies and pearls are given more value than diamonds. However, everyone realizes that in the hands of an ignorant jeweller, setting stones can be more fallacy than the science it was meant to be.

AUTO RICKSHAW METER

One of the rare products where its intuitiveness of design made it resistant to change

Date of Origin: 1977
Material: Metal

Till the electronic meters came in the 1980s, mechanical fare meters such as those used in the auto-rickshaws or taxis in Delhi were common worldwide for around a century. They consisted of two parts, a mechanical meter that measured the distance and displayed the rate and a flag that put the meter in motion (with a clockwise flick of the flag the auto-rickshaw drivers in India indicate the start of the meter). The flag also signified that the auto rickshaw was on hire. When, in the rest of the world, fare meters became electronic, to make them tamper proof they were moved inside the cab onto the vehicle's dashboard; it made sense then to drop the flag. But not in India. There were many barriers to adopt the electronic fare meter without the flag, the first of which was its expensive technology. So, India is the only country where the flag carries on, but with modifications.

A rickshaw meter is identified with its flag. Turning a flag is intuitive as it is the interaction the driver has with the meter and he can do so without looking. With the progress of design from mechanical to digital, a few companies in India, like Sansui, tried manufacturing electronic fare meters in 2010. It was not adopted due to the complex method of calculating tariffs (there were four different buttons to set the meter in four modes like in Western taxis). A static flag was an optional attachment, it glowed when the meter was in 'For Hire' mode but it was not a moving part of the whole mechanism. It was technologically advanced but lacked what in psychology is termed as 'emotional skills'. The driver couldn't 'feel' the start of his ride.

These new meters were not adapted to India as a flag was essential. But in the old meters, every time a trip was completed the driver had to twist his body in an awkward position to see the fare amount. To avoid this, a new meter was devised that was simpler than the electronic fare meter. This new meter maintained the flag but added a secondary fare display placed in such a way that the driver could easily view it.

These split flag meters have been adopted in New Delhi and are spreading all over the country. Flag meters are probably the anti-thesis of 'good' design. But how can one ignore them when close to a million auto rickshaws produced in the country every year uses them. 'Meter down' is a visual anchor signalling the start of business for the driver – like the gun-shot that starts a race, a rush of adrenalin that push buttons simply cannot provide.

135 ml

Trusted Since 1928

Babuline®

GRIPE WATER

WITHOUT ALCOHOL & ARTIFICIAL COLOUR

BENEFICIAL TO CHILDREN

Babuline is a time tested and tasty preparation being sold for over **85** years. **Babuline** is helpful for treating indigestion, flatulence and colic in children. Vomiting of curds after feed, gas and colic pain are reduced, giving your child a sense of well-being and happiness which enables it to enjoy its food, thereby making your child a strong, healthy and happy child.

Marketed in India by:

BABULINE PHARMA PVT. LTD.
406 Gulab Building
237 P D Mello Road
Mumbai-400001

® Registered Trade Mark
This Carton/Lable is also Registered
Trade Mark & Copyright

135 ml

Trusted Since 1928

Babuline®

GRIPE WATER
WITHOUT ALCOHOL & ARTIFICIAL COLOUR
BENEFICIAL TO CHILDREN

Each 5 ml contains:
Sajikhar (Sodium Bicarbonate)   45 mg
Suwa Tel (Anethum Sowa)   0.00075 ml
Variyali Tel (Pimpinella Anisum) 0.000375 ml
Jira Tel (Carum Carvi)   0.000375 ml
Pudina Sat (Menthol)   0.5 mg
Aqueous Sugar Base   q.s.

Store in a cool and dry place
Consume within 30 days after opening bottle
Shake the bottle before use

Ayurvedic Proprietary Medicine
Mfg. Lic. No. AYU/9
Batch No. :
Mfg. Date :   APK-063
Exp. Date :   NOV-16
Max. Retail   OCT-18
Price Rs. :   45.00
Incl. of all Taxes

Marketed in India by:
BABULINE PHARMA PVT. LTD.
406 Gulab Building
237 P D Mello Road, Mumbai-400001

Made in India by:
Great India Industrial and
Pharmaceutical Laboratories
19 Sun Mills Compd., Mumbai-400013

BABULINE GRIPE WATER
India's first branded gripe water to treat colic in infants

Date of Origin: 1932, Bombay
Material: Dill oil, aniseed oil, caraway oil, mint, salt

Babuline Gripe Water was one of the most popular gripe waters sold in India to treat infant colic in the first half of the nineteenth century. It had a distinctly Indian taste, as it was made of suwa tel (dill oil), variyel tel (aniseed oil), jira tel (caraway oil), pudina sat (mint), and salt. The name itself broke new ground as it married two words – one Indian, 'Babu', an endearment used for babies of both sexes, and the other English coming from the word 'alkaline'. But Babuline's primary concern was not babies; it was the movement for Indian independence.

Woodward, Babuline's competitor, was formulated in London around 1928 using easily available herbs known to assist in digestion, like aniseed, cardamom, chamomile and cinnamon bark, amongst others. Woodward was popular as much in the UK as in India, but in the 1930s the movement for swadeshi had gathered force and Gandhi had called upon Indian businessmen to create products that could be pitted against foreign brands. So Babuline was formulated not just to treat colic but, like Amrutanjan balm, as a resistance to British commodities. Its creator, Bhavanishankar Atmaram Oza, a Bombay-based Gujarati chemist, was in prison when he decided to respond to Gandhi's call by taking the formula for Babuline from a fellow inmate, an activist-doctor Jivaraj Mehta, and compounding it under the name of a firm he set up, called BA & Brothers. It was then sold in the bazaars from 1932 onwards.

Woodward tried to thwart Babuline's incursion by introducing rich calendar advertisements, such as one with an image of a bejewelled baby Krishna in a crown with peacock feathers, standing on top of the mythological serpent Kaliya Naag on one foot, holding the bottle in one hand. This obvious Hindu imagery of divinity and mythology was adopted not only by Woodward but by many other international consumer goods companies, like Glaxo. For them this was actually an oversight as they inadvertently fuelled the case for the independence of India. Babuline's response was to position its gripe water as a global product, with a 110 millilitre glass bottle packaged in a simple grey box with the logo of a baby seated on top of the globe and the name of the company written in bold at the bottom (this logo is used till date). The packaging was purposely simple as it was meant to be discarded once the bottle was opened. The success of the product provoked many copies of its packaging, so a multi-coloured packaging was designed (which is still in use). The advertisement however, mostly in Gujarati papers, had a distinct Indian identity – depicting baby Krishna and the infant Bharat, the legendary king of India.

Descendants of the Oza family in Mumbai still run Babuline gripe water, which continues to be popular despite its many spin-offs. Its popularity was partly due to the fact that it had been purposefully designed to appeal to a sense of Indian nationhood.

BAHI-KHATA

A double-entry bookkeeping system used for accounting

Date of Origin: Unknown
Material: Cloth, thread and paper

Bookkeeping in India is named after the red cloth-covered notebook, the bahi-khata that has traditionally been used by merchants across the subcontinent to record financial transactions. The word 'bahi' means a register and 'khata' refers to accounting. This double-entry bookkeeping system divides entries into receipts and debits, thus keeping a record of all transactions. The prime importance given to cash flow in the Indian system of accounting is reflected in the design of this iconic notebook.

Historians believe that the system existed before the Greek and Roman empires, and perhaps Indian traders took it to European shores. One cannot be certain except for the fact that ancient Greeks, Romans and Indians have shared knowledge of the sciences.

The bahi-khata system actually uses a number of notebooks. Transactions are first entered in the *rokad bahi* or cash book, and then posted into the *khata bahi* or ledger. A *nakal bahi* serves as a journal of record, and finally a *kacha aankada* or balance is prepared. The system uses debit and credit for maintaining the books. It is impossible to read these as everything is documented in codes that are understood and transmitted only by the trading communities. But essentially the system is the same as the modern double-entry method of accounting that is practised around the world. It differs in only one significant aspect: in the modern system nominal or temporary accounts are not posted to the ledger, because at the end of the year they are transferred to the permanent account and declared zero, but in the bahi-khata system they are transferred.

Bahi-khata books were, and still are, hand bound in red quilted cloth covers that signify the clothes of Lakshmi, the goddess of wealth. They are usually eight to ten inches wide and three- or four-feet long in folds, so the accounts can keep on 'rolling' for ease of multiple entries just like in an Excel sheet. They are kept in place with a string and often carry an image of Lakshmi and Ganesha, the god of auspicious beginnings, inside. The bahi-khata is used for a period of exactly a year till the festival of Diwali that heralds the auspicious beginnings of businesses for that year. No new entries are made on this day; they are blessed with a swastik and then re-opened on Diwali night. The notebooks traditionally had plain white paper. Over the course of time, the colour yellow and additional folds were added to the pages to help the accountant concentrate on one set of figures while tabulating.

The bahi-khata system is still used in many parts of South Asia by traditional trader and lender communities, like in the Indian states of Gujarat and Rajasthan, as also in Sindh province of Pakistan. Some areas of Andhra Pradesh, West Bengal, Jharkhand, Bihar, UP, and Tamil Nadu also prefer this system as it is considered fool-proof and confidential. Bahi-khata books have also spawned a whole new industry of cloth-covered diaries and books.

BAJAJ CHETAK

India's family scooter

Date of Origin: 1972
Material: Aluminium, steel, chrome plate, rubber, cables, oil

The Bajaj scooter was the world's only vintage scooter distinguished by an environment-friendly four-stroke engine. Though its critics have claimed that the Indian version lacked the elegance of the Vespa (its Italian parent model), the Bajaj Chetak, complete with father driving, and two children and mother riding pillion, quickly became emblematic of a certain kind of modernity that middle-class Indians in the cities aspired to.

Chetak was the white Kathiawari horse of Maharana Pratap. Stocky built and sharp eyesight, with bleeding eyes he safely carried the injured Maharana on his back in the Battle of Haldighati, where he succumbed to his injuries. His remarkable qualities of companionship were engineered into India's favourite two-wheeler.

The Bajaj Chetak had the classic Vespa styling where the chassis and body form one unit. Just like in the Vespa PX, the front panel was made large to protect the driver's legs and until 2002 it had the preferred, more powerful two-stroke engine like all scooters internationally. The Chetak was made in the factories of the 22-year-old Rahul Bajaj, who in 1960 became the Indian licensee for Vespa. By 1970, the company had produced 100,000 units and went on to become the world's fourth largest two-wheeler company. The oil crisis of 1973 helped Bajaj as cars were driven off the roads in favour of two-wheelers that were much cheaper and more fuel-efficient. In 1980 a new variant was exported to the United States. The Bajaj Champion four-stroke engine model found a market in Germany in the early 1990s.

The Vespa PX was a hit amongst the fashionable set of the 1960s, of Beatles, mini-skirts and a carefree lifestyle. However, in India it was for those who could not afford a car as yet but did not use the bicycle either. Nevertheless by 1980, a decade after its creation, the Bajaj Chetak scooter had a ten-year waiting list. Parents wanted to get one for their children when they grew up. As not enough were produced to feed the burgeoning demand of a growing nation, they would take the precaution of a double pre-booking with two different addresses in cities with low population density. Post offices served as booking centres.

The down payment was Rs 500. After a wait of nearly seven–eight years the bookings would come to term. The children too would have grown by then and reached driving age. There were tricks to shorten this wait, like the non-resident Indian or the NRI quota booking. Those with relatives overseas could open a non-resident special deposit account worth Rs 12,000 in the name of Bajaj Scooters Pimpri, Pune. The decade-long wait could thus be shortened to a year.

The original Bajaj Chetak was on the road for eighteen years with thirteen slight variants, but in the late 1990s, under the onslaught of foreign two-wheelers, Bajaj introduced new models for the first time in its history – eighteen new models with motorbike styling hit the road in eighteen months. On 9 December 2009, Bajaj finally stopped production of its scooters. So while its parent, the PX succumbed to emissions control, the Bajaj even though environmentally friendly, had to find newer avatars.

BANDHGALA

A gentleman's fashion armour

Date of Origin: 1897, Jodhpur
Material: Cashmere, wool, cotton, linen, silk

Wearing a bandhgala redeems the worth of every man. The sharp-cut sleeves, tapered torso and high-rise neck of this jacket has such strength and poise that, willingly or not, people will heed its wearer, mesmerized by what he might say or do. That is why the bandhgala is the armour of choice for men in power.

It is widely believed that the bandhgala's origins lie partly in the tradition of wearing the angarkha due to the latter's close-fitting form and embellishment on the surface – but in fact the similarities end there because the angarkha was made of very fine cloth and had a softer structure, though it was worn for formal occasions. In the mid-nineteenth century a group of young Indian aspiring men had adopted a version of the frock coat widely worn by the English at that time. This was the first time in Indian menswear that draping had been obviously discarded for a much more structured shape, accompanied by trousers and a fez cap. At the turn of the century the high-collar was defined and became a part of the Indian coat, which at this time was still long and reached the knees. This was given the name of sherwani.

Sartorial evolution was happening in the United Kingdom too in the last three decades of the nineteenth century, where a tight priest collar was being worn with short coats and the 'blazer' coat had been created for country wear. Young men open to Western fashions such as those who studied at the Aligarh Muslim University adopted the coat, trousers and brogue shoes with a fez as their daily attire. It then occurred to some in Rajasthan, particularly the Polo players who were used to wearing riding breeches and playing with the British who themselves would wear jackets, that a merging of the Western jacket and the sherwani could create a garment that would at once command both formality and Indian-ness.

The designs of the bandhgala, that are now more than a century old, thus evolved from being loosely fitted around the body to precise tailoring, closely resembling the made-to-measure Western jacket with its strength lying on the shoulder, chiselled arms, and torso. The measurements for the bandhgala are in fact more precise than the jacket as it is expected to fit almost like a second skin. The necessity of repeated trials for a close fit means that the bandhgala can only be tailored and never bought off the shelf – a feature famously offered even by the Italian luxury haberdasher Canali. In contemporary India, many other articles of men's clothing from the traditional Indian wardrobe such as the dhoti or pyjama see relatively low popularity compared to the bandhgala. This is because it looks equally elegant with jeans, Jodhpurs or pants, both the young and the older generations embrace, and it is for this reason that the bandhgala will always be cherished, making everyman feel accomplished and desired.

BANTA

A banta or marble plugs this bottle that opens with a pop

Date of Origin: 1870s, Delhi
Material: Glass, marble, water, lemon juice, sugar, black salt, cumin

Goli soda or banta is lemonade that pops when opened, and goli is the marble stuck in the bottle to hold the fizz. This corkless bottle, called the Codd-neck bottle (after its creator Hiram Codd), is a late-nineteenth-century design made in the UK, but it is India that gave the drink hundreds of flavours and an indelible connection to youth, playfulness, taste and patriotism. Goli soda or banta is also how a whole generation in India remembers their childhood, and banta is considered the drink of the nation because the pop, the place and the taste are considered definitively Indian.

The most common kind of banta is made with lemon juice, ice and sugar, a pinch of black salt and cumin seeds, thus giving an international lemon soda an Indian flavour through the addition of spices. Though this is the mother recipe that unites the entire country, it is called banta in the north and goli in the south, and there are many regional and local variations too. For example in Mangalore, there are several versions with different names: 'nannari' if it is made with ginger, 'impto' when it has more of a cola flavour, 'chappe' if it is without spice, and simply 'colour soda' if it has red, blue or yellow colour added to it.

Goli soda sellers pass down the street inadvertently making music with their dozens of moss coloured glass bottles jangling with goli marbles. The symphony announces their arrival and it's perfectly timed – for when the school ends, thirsty kids flock to this mobile watering hole loving the freshness of fizzy lemonade and the playful pop that the glass stopper makes with the soda's effervescent pressure. The pop of this marble announces relief from the cruel sun in the summer months.

Banta sellers are one-man entrepreneurs who make the drink on the spot on their pushcarts or 'thelas' by pumping gas in upside down water bottles. The bottle can be opened with an opener but diehard fans prefer to push it down with their finger as it pops. The more the gas, the louder is the pop. The marble fixed at the bottleneck makes them re-usable. The bottles are simply washed after use, and the rubber ring, which holds the marble in place, is replaced. As its fans and bloggers, 'The Sip of Life Team', say, 'if you are a true Indian at heart, pop one before you die'.

BARTAN

Utensils in the Indian kitchen designed for cooking, storing, serving

Date of Origin: 2700 BCE, Harappa civilization
Material: Brass, copper, steel and other metals

In the pre-Vedic period, three pots signifying heaven, earth and a mythological underworld were part of rituals. These ancient utensils gave rise to utensils for daily use. Some, like the deep, rimmed patila used for boiling milk, exist since the later Vedic period and were used both in temples and homes for the same purpose. This combination of the sacred and the profane is what gave shape to the Indian kitchen, and thus makes it unique. Their designs combined both decorative and utilitarian elements, and are used for cooking, storing and serving.

Patilas are made without handles and necessitate the most ingenious of kitchen tools, the *pakad*. A *pakad* hooks the rim and therefore lifting requires much less effort. Patilas come in many sizes and a *pakad* is the unique solution for handling all of them.

The large varieties of bartans that are the pride of most households today were first designed in the Bronze Age. Bowls, cups, plates, and dishes in many materials such as stone, copper, bronze, terracotta, and even gold and silver, came into being. Metal utensils were preferred over earthen ones because there was a sense of decoration and shine. Ornamental versions were reserved for worship and simpler ones for domestic use. This tradition of gleam, another hallmark of Indian kitchens, was not out of a competitive spirit with the neighbour's kitchen, but because only the best was served to god and thus scrubbed to enhance its beauty. A third variety called Ganga-Jamuni is made of

brass and copper fused together, used for both cooking and serving.

Some utensils made for rituals, using materials such as brass and bell metal, were therapeutic. Brass work from Benares was particularly prized, its surface decorated with an iron graver and shaped with a simple hammer. The surface of these utensils is beaten for a non-stick finish, which is so beautiful that designers of contemporary gold jewellery have even adopted this technique to create ornaments. When they start acquiring a patina they are sent to the pounder who melts and re-shapes them into new utensils. The surface of these utensils is purposely beaten so that food does not stick, a finish that exists in aluminium utensils around the world, but in India is also characteristic of gold jewellery. This technique along with surface decorations has been found in utensils in north India dating to the Kusana period 1 century–3 century CE.

In 1978, when the government deregulated the stainless steel industry, many entrepreneurs started recycling stainless steel scrap to use as domestic utensils. In the eighties and nineties, 80 per cent of the steel produced in the country was made into utensils. So, while steel represented modernity and ushered in a new material, the forms themselves used for thousands of years remained unchanged, as did the shiny surface that is the hallmark of a well-loved Indian kitchen.

BICHIYA
An ornament for the toes

Date of Origin: Unknown
Material: Iron, gold, silver, brass, titanium, copper

This is a simple adjustable ring designed to settle neatly around the second toe of the foot. Similar to a wedding ring, toe rings are a marker of marriage for Hindu women. They are gifted to brides by their in-laws at the end of the haldi ceremony, a pre-wedding ritual. The earliest reference to these ornaments is in the *Ramayana* when Sita took off her toe ring and threw it on the ground as a message to Ram that she was being abducted by Ravana.

While each culture eroticizes a certain part of the body, in India, with its 5,000-year-old code for male and female beauty that is laid down in the Kamasutra, every single part of the body is revered. This includes the eyes, the hair, and most importantly, the feet, where the Kamasutra prescribes the application of a balm made of white and blue lotuses, rose chestnuts, plum, cinnamon and honey to make the wearer lucky in love. Erotic love was never precluded in marriage. If anything, it was seen as an essential ingredient of a good marriage. Hence the profusion of ornaments for every part of a woman's body.

Bichiyas are often made of silver with traditional symbols of marriage and fertility like flowers and conch shells embossed onto them. The rings are worn in sets, on the second toe of both feet. The length of this toe makes it easy to slip on where it sits comfortably because of the gap between the big toe and the second toe. This point is called the L3 point by accupressurists. Pressing it relieves cramps, headaches, nerves, stress and shortness of breath. Though this link has never been made overtly, it is possible, even probable, that the rings were designed to be therapeutic. Traditionally men too wear a ring on the big toe for curative purposes, or simply for virility. In a more elaborate gesture, bichiyas can also be worn simultaneously on all toes, in which case they have many other names such as *challa* or angoothi. This style is prevalent amongst the nomads of Rajasthan and Gujarat, where this tradition originated from and spread to most of the communities through north and east India. Their forms might vary but they all symbolize a married status.

Starting with the hippies in the 1970s and the raves of the 1990s, silver jewellery from India started attracting attention internationally, as it was beautiful, affordable and accentuated parts of the body such as the nose, ankles and toes, a form of ornamentation unkown to the Western world. Bichiyas quickly became popular and many celebrities from Madonna to Jennifer Anniston have been spotted wearing them while walking down the red carpet and or on vacation by the beach.

BINDI

An evolving cultural symbol kept up to date with simple adhesive and fabric

Date of Origin: 2 CE
Material: Vermillion powder, sandalwood paste, flock velvet fabric, adhesive

When it comes to Indian-ness, nothing is more iconic than the bindi. Synonymous with femininity in the subcontinent, the bindi is worn between the eyebrows, a place considered to be the site of the sixth chakra, or seat of infinite wisdom. Derived from the Sanskrit bindu, which means dot, drop or point, the bindi has many meanings. For some, the bindi is no more than a sign of marriage and a symbol of auspiciousness. For others, the bindi refers to the sixth chakra. In Tantric texts the bindi is worn at the body's focal junction of mystic vitality and the exit point of a person's kundalini energy. This point is believed to also protect wearers from evil and misfortune. But in general it is the non-Indians who worry about what the bindi signifies, for its wearers, the bindi requires no explanation.

In a singular vision, the bindi is the artistic signature of Bharti Kher, one of India's most prominent contemporary artists, who uses this powerful emblem to shape her work. In *The Skin Speaks a Language Not its Own*, Kher's evocative, painstakingly detailed sculpture of a lifelike elephant, either dead or asleep, is covered in thousands of tiny white spermatozoid-shaped bindi dots. In this context, the bindi is Bharti's medium for manifesting sensuality, sexuality, identity, displacement, and feminism – leitmotifs of today's Indian society. Powerful women like politician Sushma Swaraj and writers like Shobha De have made it their trademark.

There is no rule for the bindi except that it must be worn in the centre of the forehead between the eyebrows, neither too high nor low. The bindi can be shaped out of a fragrant sandalwood paste or simple velvet slivers with adhesive for easy application. Married Indian women are known to wear a red bindi; infants, children and single women wear black; and widows traditionally wear none. While it is customary for foreheads to be adorned with dots, individuality allows bindis to be worn in an array of sizes, colours, shapes and design. For pretty young urbanites it could be a simple fashion accessory. It compliments any outfit or occasion but is unacceptable with denim. Swarovski bindis compliment ready-to-wear saris and salwar kameezes and diamond ones are usually reserved for very special occasions like marriages.

As tradition inspires fashion and fashion blurs into art, the bindi has acquired many interesting contemporary interpretations. Madonna and Gwen Stefani have made it rock chic. And while gender worldwide continues to struggle with the combination of power and beauty, in modern India the country's power women are known to wear big, red bindis with near-evangelical fidelity. As writer Shobha De affirms, the bindi is 'the mark of the Alpha woman in an Indian context'.

BPL STUDYLITE

A haloed lamp that shines through power cuts

Date of Origin: 2012, Bangalore, now Bengaluru
Material: LED light, metal

The onset of summer is usually accompanied by sweltering heat and power cuts. For the millions of schoolgoing children this means the struggle to study or do their homework in the evenings. The BPL Studylite lamp was born out of this need for light in the inevitability of long power cuts in the summer. Designed especially for children, the lamp is the first of its kind that gives six hours of uninterrupted light after its solar battery is charged for two hours in the sunlight. It does not heat up the illuminated area and it is playfully shaped in a circle to resemble a halo, such as those depicted around the heads of saints. This 'halo' casts a soft light. The project is unique in its collaborative effort between the designers Studio ABD, its manufacturer BPL, while bringing in the expertise of a specialized eye care hospital.

The most important aspect of designing a lamp is the quality of light. For the design of this one, the designers reached out to one of India's leading eye care hospital chains, the Sankara Nethralaya, that shared inputs on optimum luminosity for a study lamp. Power cuts can run into several hours at a time when it is not uncommon for children to study for 10–12 hours during exams. Since it was very likely that there wouldn't be electricity to recharge the batteries, solar technology had to be integrated into the lamp. So the lamp needs to be charged for two hours in sunlight or using direct power for every six hours of continuous battery use.

Twenty-five LED bulbs were used, the choice of LED over other materials was not just because they are sturdy, but they cut down on UV or IR heat rays that damage the eyes. Furthermore, their illuminated area is generous, consisting of a primary task area (1.25 feet X 1.25 feet) and a secondary area of another 2.2 square feet. Moreover, LED lights have very little heat loss, reducing the danger of having hot surfaces around children. The lights are in a covered groove that provides flicker and strain-free reading with no exposure to the bright spots of LEDs.

The lamp comes in five playful colours, borrowed from red, yellow and blue M&M's, a big departure from other industrial lamps that exist in the market. The colour black was for the fastidious parent and the white one is every product designer's whim. Because it uses rechargeable solar battery cells, it is portable and easy to travel with. Just after its launch the lamp won the prestigious German RedDot design award in 2010 for its eco-friendly seamless design. It is also the only product proudly stamped 'Designed and Made in India'.

CH-4 CHAIR

India's first modernist workspace chair with steel tubing

Date of Origin: 1958, Bombay
Material: Steel, wood and cane

The CH-4 chair was a groundbreaking piece of innovation, not only in its cantilevered one-piece frame, when most chairs usually had four legs, but also in its use of steel that ushered in a completely new material for the construction of chairs. This chair is what transformed India's old offices into modern spaces, which had been using only heavy wooden furniture. At the turn of the twentieth century, Godrej, the company that had successfully established a niche in the furniture industry with steel almirahs and patented foolproof safes, started modernizing India's officescape by replacing wooden furniture with steel. By the early 1950s, Godrej had successfully introduced a gamut of new designs for tables, office partitions, shelves, cupboards, and of course the iconic CH-4 chair.

This transformation had its roots in Prime Minister Jawaharlal Nehru's vision of Modern India, which resulted in the 1951 collaboration with Le Corbusier to design Chandigarh, the first planned city of India. Nehru made Chandigarh the national symbol of freedom and modernity. To express freedom in every aspect of life, Indian Modernism was further developed in the use of modernist architecture for the construction of homes, cars and even steel factories. Seizing the opportunity, Godrej adopted Nehru's vision and commissioned India's first modernist workspace – the offices of Madhya Pradesh State Electricity Board. Amongst the chairs, tables and partitions, the CH-4 chair alone became iconic. In design and function, the CH-4 epitomized the 'less is more' aesthetic and sold millions of units.

Made from electricity-resistant welded steel tubing, the CH-4 is cantilever in shape with a teak and plastic cane seat and back rest. It was initially available in olive green with black wood elements and was lightweight and elegant in design. Launched in 1958, it did not make headlines but was placed in every office in the country. Further additions to the design included arm rests and office tables also in bent tubular steel.

Its inspiration was the Bauhaus designer Marcel Breuer's 1925 Wassily chair, which first used bent tubular steel and canvas, as well as his 1928 Thonet chair fashioned from tubular metal and wood – the novel cantilevered principle of support requiring two rather than the traditional four legs for support. The CH-4 chair was similar but indigenously produced; the first models were with teak trimmings along the arms and the backrest. While the difference in its design was minimal, it revolutionized the office furniture industry, moving it away from the use of natural materials to the use of mass-produced industrial materials, minimalist styling and advanced manufacturing techniques. Steel meant evolution, steel was modern and it was essential to the industrialization of India.

Furniture design has since then moved from modernist to post-modernist, using wire, corian and fibreglass. Godrej, too, has expanded its furniture collection, but the CH-4 chair continues to be produced and remains popular because its design has undergone much ergonomic evolution, like following the curve of the back or introducing the swivel.

CHAIDAAN

A tea caddy designed to carry tea or chai on a rainy day

Date of Origin: Unknown
Material: Wrought iron, metal wire, bamboo

The tea caddy is essential to India's street culture. Known simply as a 'chai holder', it is a mobile holder fashioned out of metal with cylindrical compartments for carrying fluted glasses of tea. India is the world's largest drinker of tea and the tea caddy is the most important conduit for delivering steaming hot chai to the neighbourhood offices and shops throughout the working day. Chai being the drink that links a disparate and chaotic nation.

The simplest ones are woven from wire and shaped like a basket with many compartments into which the glass can slide into. When they aren't simple wire weaves, they are moulded out of iron strips that fit like a glove around every glass. Its simplicity in anyway does not diminish how remarkably well the object functions. Its makers are masters of flexibility, fashioning holders at a very short notice for two to twelve glasses and sometimes even more. The glasses are not necessarily laid side by side but sometimes in a pyramid form, which makes it compact and avoids spilling while carrying.

The origin of the design is unknown, but it is ubiquitous. Roadside tea stalls cannot function without tea caddies.

On an average a chaiwala plays host to over three hundred people a day. At the Golden Temple in Amritsar thirty thousand cups of tea are served free every hour. Chaiwalas simply take orders on their mobile phones while chai delivery boys run over to deliver chai on the wire rim tea caddy. In Mumbai, often young boys wade through waist-deepwater transporting steaming glasses of chai during the monsoons. The 2009 film *Ek Cutting Chai* is the story of one such boy.

The chai-on-the-street has even developed a hybrid vocabulary of its own: for example, one half of a fluted glass of tea is an ek cutting chai. Chai 'regulars' use this vocabulary to distinguish themselves from the 'tourists'. In fact in the film *Ek Cutting Chai* a maid, whose balcony overlooks a tea stall, falls in love with Chotu the chaiwala. It's a simple story of how life unfurls at its wittiest and nicest around a cup of tea. Typically, boys like Chotu deliver tea within a five-hundred-metre radius around them. An average of thirty litres or five hundred cups is drunk everyday at each chaiwala. Each chaiwala's station is an example of what makes India the world's largest entrepreneurial nation and the tea industry its second largest employer.

CHAKLA-BELAN

A rolling pin with an accompanying board to flatten the dough and make perfect rotis

Date of Origin: 7500–6000 BCE, Parsam-ka-khera
Material: Wood, stone

Rolling wheat dough to a perfectly flat round shape requires great skill and a uniform application of pressure. To flatten dough to perfection, wooden rolling pins are used world over. But the Indian rolling pin or belan is unique because it is always accompanied by a flat round mounted board, the chakla. It is only a combination of these two that creates the perfect kit on which wheat dough is laid out thrice a day, flattened, rolled and then cooked on fire to make a perfectly round roti.

Wheat and barley have been the principal cereals since the Harappan civilization. Excavations have yielded both the chakla and belan. The origin of the chakla and belan, though conjectural, is widely believed to be in the most fertile belt of the country – Punjab – around 6500 BCE. At the time, this region was cultivating wheat and barley extensively. Rather than using the flatness of the chakla and the pressure of the belan to what we might expect to be used around the country to make flatbread, whatever the ingredient might be, it is only in this region of north India that the chakla and belan were used simply because wheat and barley lend themselves to kneading. What must have been perceived as a high-technology kitchen tool then, the chakla and belan soon spread to other parts of the country.

The chakla helped provide a flat surface on what would have been an uneven beaten earth floor on which all cooking was done. Though urban India no longer cooks on earth floors, this practice of using both the chakla and belan has remained unchanged through the centuries.

The design and material of the chakla and belan too are unchanged. The chakla's thick circular flat top is supported on three 'feet', whereas the belan is one single unbroken circular block with tapering ends. Belan is usually wooden, whereas the chakla can be made of wood, granite, soapstone, or marble. The most common wooden ones are made with a simple chisel, file and planers. A recent innovation of the chakla and belan, an electric hotplate with a press, proved unpopular as it functions only at a very specific level of humidity in the dough, which is difficult to achieve as dough is hand-kneaded. So, even today the chakla and belan is ever present in both private and professional kitchens as rotis continue to be hand rolled, as was done a few thousand years ago.

CHARKHA

The spinning wheel that was a symbol of Indian Independence

Date of Origin: 500–1000 CE
Material: Wood

India is known for the finest cotton textiles in the world. Factory-made cloth that resulted in weavers going bankrupt in the early twentieth century made the symbol of hand-made cotton thread and the charkha one of the most iconic objects of modern India. The figure of a person spinning a charkha became a matter of national identity and in 1931 when India adopted its first flag – a charkha was placed at its centre.

Etymologically, the word charkha comes from the Persian word meaning wheel. It is one of the oldest hand-spinning devices comprising a wooden drive wheel, manually turned, and a spindle. Cotton is spun by hand on the tip of this spindle. Shilpashastris or master carpenters manufactured the charkha using acacia, neem, shisham, and even sandalwood, which were legendary and prized for their fragrance. It was then lovingly painted and decorated with metal and glasswork to give each charkha a unique identity. Charkhas were placed in every courtyard of a joint family where women would spin together while singing hymns.

Yarns spun on the charkha were of varying thickness and uses. Finer yarns were reserved for clothes and the coarser ones for blankets. Old or damaged woollens could be shredded and fluffed up in bales. The bales would then be spun into a thick yarn on the charkha to make 'khes', a fine sheet usually placed on top of a cotton dhurrie to sleep on. Women from poorer households would spin these for sale.

For centuries, spinning as an activity had united the country, transcending regional, caste, class, language and religious diversities as most homes in India used to practise spinning. The charkha also became a symbol of economic independence. It was in the 1920s that Mahatma Gandhi and other members of the Indian nationalist movement adopted this symbol: spinning on charkhas became a practice to assert the desire for self-rule.

The charkha in use then was a standing charkha. This charkha wasn't very practical because it could not be carried, so the residents of Gandhi's Sabarmati Ashram invented a 'box charkha'. The two standing wheels were shrunk and laid flat in a box of approximately sixty by thirty centimetres. It consisted of both the wheels and the shafts they were on, space for stocking a spindle, a bobbin to collect the yarn, and a small wooden stand on which the spindle could turn. Especially designed to be easily carried, it weighed just over a kilo.

The standing charkha is useful in weaving thicker threads and the box charkha for finer ones. Every one thousand metres woven is referred to as a 'gundi', sufficient to make a handkerchief.

CHARPAI
A multi-purpose transportable hand-woven bed

Date of Origin: Before 1300 CE
Material: Wood, newar cotton tape, jute string

A bed is just one of the ways to use a charpai. In India, as necessity often takes precedence over love of the object, the charpai morphs into a lounge seat for daytime discussions or even as an extension of the kitchen, as a sun platform for drying food. Ibn Battuta on his travel to India in the fourteenth century remarked, 'The beds in India are very light ... [it] consists of four conical legs on which four staves are laid; between they plait a sort of ribbon of silk or cotton. When you lie on it you need nothing else to render the bed sufficiently elastic.'[5]

This elasticity of purpose seems to carry over to the actual weaving of the charpai itself. New charpais arrive dismantled as long sticks to make an open wooden frame, four legs, and metres of cord, all separate, and are built on the spot. This cord is woven either from simple rushes or a thick canvas rope called navar. The frame is fitted into the legs using mortise and tenon joints, a system of joinery that does not use nails and makes the structure strong yet flexible. A specialized cord weaver then creates an 'interlaciato' weave over and under the frame connecting the four sides of the frame in a tight web, giving it strength. This weaving can be either straight or diagonal. The cord is woven densely at the part that serves as the head and left loose at the base. Decorative patterns with the cords vary by region and maker but they are strung to be strong, supple and comfortable. This porous surface is also what makes it an ideal seat for hot, tropical climates.

Charpais come in many forms. The bedposts range from simple wooden ones to elaborately turned ones, in brightly painted lac or gold and silver inlay in steel or copper. The charpai is one of the few objects of furniture indigenous to India and was also offered as a gift. Precious woods such as sandalwood and ebony were used by the nobility who gave exquisite charpais in silver filigree to visiting dignitaries.[6]

In rural India, homes are large communal spaces without specific functions attributed to individual rooms. The same room could be a bedroom in winter or a living room in summer. Sleeping is communal. Especially in summer when many families come out in the same large open space with clusters of charpais set out near each home. In winter, the beds are moved to one of the rooms inside. Whatever the season, charpais are laid out at night and removed in the morning, as part of the daily routine. During daytime the verandas became the repository of charpais standing on their sides. For kids these cots are playthings, drape a bed sheet on the wooden frame and it becomes a tent or a palace or a cave – the possibilities are endless.

CHIKS

Bamboo blinds that delicately veil the sunlight

Date of Origin: Unknown
Material: Bamboo splits, cloth strings, wood

Chiks are characteristic of the tropics as they let the air and slivers of sunlight through. Chiks or blinds work better than curtains, because unlike curtains they filter sunlight rather than block it.

Direct light that enters through the top one third of a window frame brings in both light and heat at the same time. This makes chiks indispensable in the sunny latitudes of India, as their length can be altered to allow just enough light during daytime without the stifling heat.

However, this adjustability is not limited only to their length. In India, each wall opening is of a different size, so they are handmade locally on demand to fit every window and door opening. Chiks are made of bamboo splits or fine sarkanda wefts stitched together with cotton warps in a pattern. These tropical materials make them elegant. The chik-makers who come home to take measurements offer to stitch them in three different designs that they refer to as 'Barfi', 'Gilas' and 'Choodi'. 'Barfis' are diamond shaped, 'choodi' is a hexagonal design, and 'gilas' resembles a drinking goblet. They all have the effect of fine latticework when light filters through them.

Once stitched, dyeing the chiks and the cotton thread in various colours adds beauty to the room. Cloth or a thick tape is used as piping on all sides and sometimes even as lining. For rooms that receive too much sunlight, muslin cloth is used as a backing that helps block direct sunlight even more. Once made, chiks are strung on the window with a simple pulley system to regulate their length.

As size is not a barrier, chiks are also used in large commercial spaces like shops. The largest chiks hang in the oldest markets in Delhi. Chiks hanging here block the sun and also the rain. To protect surfaces from rain, chiks are backed with thick waterproof material. Chiks are one of the simplest objects but their popularity continues as they are organic, handmade and bespoke. And the fact that chik-makers are at every street corner in most urban areas of the country where they arrange all their samples on the trees with advertisement ensures that chik making will stay a perennial craft form in the country. One could take the chiks anywhere in the world but its essential tropical coolness stays a constant.

CHIMTA-TAVA

The tongs and pan that adorn every Indian kitchen

Date of Origin: 2 BCE
Material: Sheet iron, cast iron, sheet steel or aluminium

'Only the courageous can jump into fire', says Hamid, the poor orphan boy in Premchand's story 'Idgah', of his newly bought pair of chimtas. Hamid and his grandmother, for whom this is meant to be a gift, are poor and have almost no objects in their home. Hamid's grandmother Amina needs a chimta. Each time she roasts chapatis, she burns her fingers. When he gifts it to her after coming back from the fair, where he has been with his friends to celebrate Id, she breaks down and cries at the thoughtfulness of such a young child, whose friends were busy enjoying rides, toys and cold drinks while he was thinking of his grandmother's hands.

Chimtas are used for cooking directly on fire. When sufficiently dry but still raw, the chimta is used to grip the chapati and hold it over a flame that cooks it making it ready to eat. Roasting chapatis on both sides would otherwise be impossible.

Cooking chapatis needs a kit. Firstly a tava or iron griddle: this is also one of the oldest of utensils. The first examples of the chimta were excavated at the Harappan sites (2700–2000 BCE). Tava's use even then, like today, was to roast unleavened bread. Its flat and round rimless shape allows the roti to be flipped with the chimta for even cooking on both sides. This design was optimal for the country's staple diet, so its use remains unchanged over centuries.

Chimtas and tavas are the simplest tools in the Indian kitchen and also the oldest, both being made out of a single piece of iron. While the tava is flat, the chimta is pressed into a U-shape. Indents at the back of the U-shape serve both as a grip to hold while using as well as resistance to keep the tongs in shape.

Serving roasted rotis in a box is also equally historic – walled containers with a round lid were used to offer rotis to divinities; the boxes were made of earth and were the same size and form as the metal ones used today. But, amongst all the utensils dedicated to the roti, it's the chimta that is the most indispensable.

The beauty of the chimta and the tava lie in the fact that despite decades of use, wear and burn is invisible except for a few warps that can be easily pounded back into shape by the ironsmiths who make them. Even now chimtas and tavas continue to be made by hand and not in factories. While Indian kitchens have moved on from iron to stainless steel and non-stick cookware, these two stay as they were. Though some non-stick tavas are available now, the chimta needs no further improvement. In Hamid and Amina's otherwise spartan home, it was also the only precious object.

CHOTI

A cape with embellishments for long hair

Date of Origin: Unknown
Material: Hair with extensions in silk, synthetic fibres and wool; precious stones and flowers

There are some truly original forms of embellishing the hair, which emphasize its beauty so much that the natural beauty of the hair becomes invisible. The choti is an example of this; often flowers are used to create a halo-like appearance of the hair, which extends into a long plait till the hips – the idealized vision and version of a woman's hair, larger than life, long and imposing. Some of these chotis are bejewelled, treated like exquisite ornaments particularly in south India. They use precious stones like rubies, emeralds and diamonds embedded in gold. These are the chotis made by jewellers, such as the one who was the jeweller to the Maharaja of Mysore and cost upwards of a few million dollars. That's the kind of reverence Indian jewellery art has for the hair.

At its simplest the choti can have a hair pendant or an extension plaited on to the end of the hair in elaborate tassels and small bells. These tassels could be made of silk, synthetic fibres or wool and are meant to imitate the plait. So they come in a bunch of three that are worn as an extension from the natural plait. These are often known as the paranda from the Persian word parand, or bird referring to the movement of the hair or Garuda, the celestial bird.[7]

It's in the deep south and high north of the country that the celebration of hair reaches its peak. In Ladakh, where there is the richest tradition of chotis, the Ladakhi women wear a head piece called a perak that extends down on the back right till their feet. The perak is almost like a cape and is made of large pieces of turquoise, surrounded by coral and gold elements embroidered on leather, the largest of which will be placed in the middle of the forehead just above the eyebrows. Laid in descending order depending on their size, the smallest will reach above the hips over the back, following which the perak is finished off in leather and fur. As its materials suggest the perak is not only an ornament, its cape protects its wearer from cold. The wealth of its turquoise, coral and gold meant that the perak was quite obviously a family heirloom passed amongst the women of the family who would add on their turquoise. Ladakh's worship of the snake as a deity through Buddhist traditions fed into the design of their caplet head ornaments that when worn gives the appearance of a poised snake.[8]

CHOTU KOOL REFRIGERATOR

A portable refrigerator with extremely low power consumption

Date of Origin: 2009, Maharashtra
Material: Metal, plastic

Products for rural-dwellers are often re-designed to cost less but are rarely innovative. The Godrej 'Chotu Kool' was a well-designed innovation that brought chill to rural areas – a feat unthinkable in regions where power supply is often interrupted. The legendary portable refrigeration unituses super performant insulation to keep products cool for hours without power. Like an ice-box it opens from the top pushing down cold air and reducing heat loss. It is ingeniously made of only twenty parts, compared to a regular fridge with more than two hundred parts. Thanks to the 'Chotu Kool', urban poor and rural families can keep their food fresh. Women no longer have to go to the market everyday and they also save money by reducing food wastage.

The Chotu Kool was a success also because it was designed after a series of interactions with a population that had never owned a refrigerator but would have liked to. The project to design the Chotu Kool began in 2006 with a Godrej workshop in rural India. Three-and-a-half years of discussions between the Godrej in-house 'disruptive innovation' design team and village groups resulted in this joint collaborative effort. The villagers' most pressing basic need was a compact cooling machine (since most of them lived in homes with an area of around 15 square metres) that could store, especially when they had visitors, a few litres of water and up to four kilogrammes of vegetables.

In the Chotu Kool, in place of the standard fridge compressor, a thermoelectric chip is used. This chip was cheap, compact and worked on a 24-volt power input. Chotu Kool's advantage is that it can operate on a battery when there is no electricity and yet lowers the temperature enough to store milk, vegetables and leftover cooked food at twenty degrees below the outside ambient temperature. It makes no ice though.

The Godrej Chotu Kool comes in two compact sizes of 30 and 43 litres that both weigh under nine kilogrammes. Priced affordably within Rs 4,000, it is available in two shades of blue and red – the ruby red was chosen unanimously by six hundred women in a survey.

Launched in 2009, like all successful products, it did not stop just at innovative technology. It went further by creating a direct-selling distribution system partnering with the very women who co-created it. The designers extended micro-finance to assist in the initial investment of setting up demo-centers and giving them the possibility of being entrepreneurs. This unique project that combines a plug-and-play ice-box technology with an active participation by its end-users won it a gold medal in the social impact category of the 2012 Edison Award, an American award honouring the best in global innovation.

CHUDIYAN

A way of wearing both wealth and beauty on wrists

Date of Origin: 2500 BCE, Mohenjodaro
Material: Glass, lac, various metals, wood, plastic, sea shells

The 4,500-year-old statuette of the Dancing Girl of Mohenjo-Daro, with her arms covered with bangles, found at the Harappa excavation site, embodies confidence and grace. For Indian women, these simple bangles transcend adornment and are a unique form of self-expression: when presented to a bride in a box, it is a symbol of marriage.

In the past, before banks and paper money appeared, bangles were an essential part of a woman's dowry, because quite literally, they kept the wealth in the woman's hands. Jewellery in the Harappan era was a marker of a women's high position in society. This tradition of expressing subtle power through jewels is still very much evident, as even today, Indian women remain the world's largest buyers of gold. But bangles also highlight the delicate wrists of a girl, making them an important beauty accessory, and are loved by all women, rich and poor.

The dazzling Laad Bazaar in historic Hyderabad sells bangles ranging from simple glass ones to those studded with fifty-six-facet rose-cut diamonds, a cutting unique to India. The much coveted kundan bangles are made with semi-precious stones, such as tourmalines closely placed on a bed of gold leaf inserted between the walls of the bangle for a much desired, imperfect and joyous effect.

Most of these glass bangles are made in Firozabad, 50 kilometres from the Taj Mahal, where men called gulliwalas scoop molten glass from large, circular coal-fire melting surfaces. Cool molten is cut into thin bangle shapes and then joined, polished and decorated. Every year records an increase in the number of people who work in this industry, as bangles undergo design changes that reflect the latest trends. The initial four colours of red, green, gold and blue have given way to every colour in the spectrum. Most women own a lot of these simple bangles that at home are lined up on special bangle holders made of painted wood, or simply, and ingeniously, on the long arm of a clothes hanger.

Lac bangles are a favourite among Indian women. Lac is a protective shell-like secretion of the female lac insect, which is set on a metal bangle frame. The lac bangles come in deep, rich, psychedelic colours, studded with glass pieces, stones and beads, called naqqashi. The excitement is to buy a bangle without any decoration and then the naqqashi artist customizes it as desired with decoration and in a size that fits just right on the wrist, not too loose neither too snug, the whole made-to-order process lasting just under fifteen minutes. Thus, bangles are never dusty or outdated in style. They are a tribute to fashion that is forever relevant.

CHULHA
An earthen stove for cooking

Date of Origin: Unknown
Material: Earthen clay, bricks, wood

For centuries everything about cooking was an ordeal, especially the heavy smoke that necessitated an outdoor kitchen. Cooking in most Indian kitchens happened on coal or wood fireplaces in the courtyard in the front or back of the houses, a floor-plan style that existed since the Harappan period, but later kitchens were incorporated within the house. At that time the Janta stove became hugely popular because its appearance coincided with the modernization of Indian lifestyles, and so it even became iconic, a symbol of this change. In the villages, the kitchen was incorporated inside the home, where both the chulha and the Janta stove began to cause a very high incidence of fatal accidents due to fire and inhalation of smoke.

This is the reason why a large number of designers, NGOs and energy research institutes joined hands to create a variety of new chulhas. Many designs have made it to the market and the Pune-based NGO ,Appropriate Rural Technology Institute (ARTI) and the multinational Philips made one of the most popular ones called the Saral Stove. In 2005, a design team from Philips Design Pune prototyped and tested this chulha with the help of NGOs, self-help groups and families that would eventually use it. This new chulha is smokeless and fuel-efficient as it consumes lesser wood than before.

Mostly women, for whom it has become an added source of revenue, make it in homes and also provide after-sales service. A rectangular frame of metal is built perpendicular to the floor that has been dug up. Two bricks are laid out horizontally on a mixture of clay and cow dung on which two metallic receptacles, one deeper for large dishes and the other shallower, are laid out side by side and connected with metallic hollow pipes. The opening for placing the firewood is below the larger opening. Once the clay is dry all the metal pieces that served as shapes for the various elements of the chulha are slowly removed. The chimney is built on the side in clay and brick, from where the smoke escapes through the exhaust pipe. It takes just a few hours to make this. The smoke is reduced, it cooks fast and prepares food for about fifteen to forty people at a time, depending on the size of the chulha. Ash and soot are cleaned regularly from the base of the stoves and the chimney.

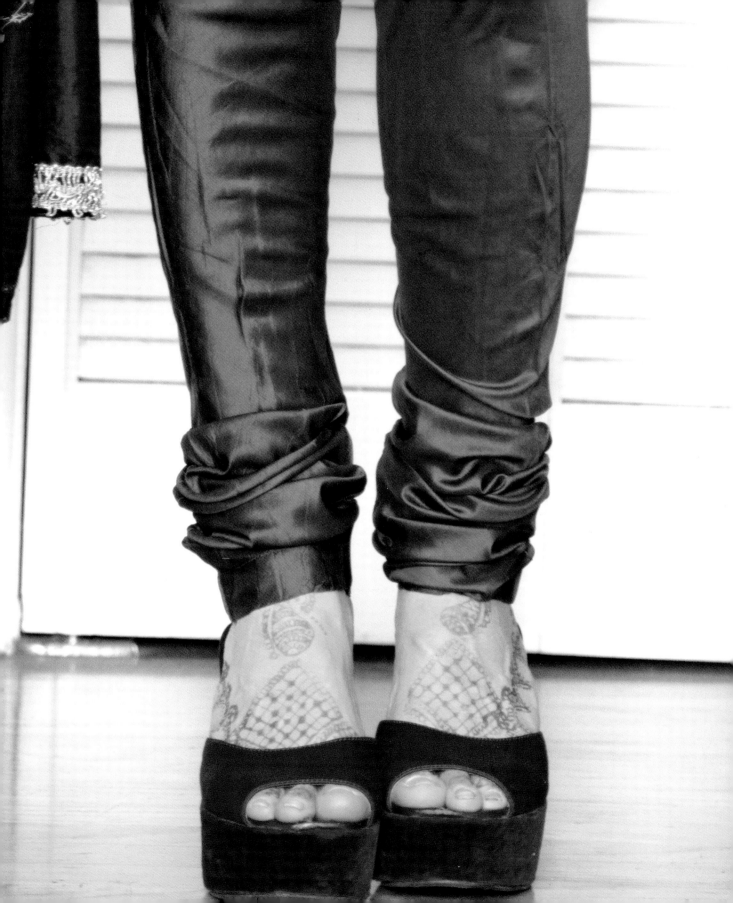

CHURIDAR

The unisex trouser, precursor to the breeches

Date of Origin: Around 1600 CE
Material: Cotton, silk, linen, lycra

The tapered legs of the churidar are a global fashion favourite. Its tightness accentuates the legs by making them seem longer and shapelier, something that every man or woman, short or tall, desires. It is one of the rare articles of clothing that was created unisex at the outset, which inspired further inventions – a precursor to skin-tight jeans and a prototype of the Jodhpur breeches.

It is unknown exactly when the churidar came into existence. The Mughul court, forever conscious of trends and outdoing each other with the latest fashions, gave length and style to the original shorter breeches that their ancestors wore. It was cut as close to the leg as possible. In order to slip such tight trousers on, cutting it at a bias was necessary to give the feel of stretch in the fabric while pulling it over the leg. Ankle jewellery has always been part of body decoration in India. It was worn to enhance the beauty of the feet. The two, together, would have created the churidar.

The French art historian Auguste Racinet, in his work on international historic costume, sketched and described clothes from sixteenth-century Mughul India, which needed a lining due to the lightness and fineness of the fabric. So both men and women wore tight trousers as underwear. Miniature paintings in Rajput and Mughul style from the sixteenth century also paint churidars as lining to outer clothing.

In time the churidar became an outer garment. The top was the angarkha, an outfit with a fitted blouse on the torso that fell as a skirt below the waist. The churidar made of the same material or simple white cotton was worn below, no longer as an undergarment but in an ensemble with the angarkha. Churidar became the new sartorial style established by the court and in its simple white version continues to be worn till today both by nomadic tribes in Gujarat and Rajasthan and urban tribes who buy them at leading Indian stores.

The tapered leg of the churidar also led to the creation of another important fashion favourite, the Jodhpur pants or riding breeches. The city of Jodhpur in Rajasthan had a polo team, the Jodhpur Lancers, with Sir Pratap Singh of Jodhpur as captain. They had played and won many tournaments throughout 1897. Once, while sailing to the UK, the ship carrying Pratap Singh's luggage sank, and he arrived in London clothes less. Lady Roseberry got the ex-prime minister Lord Roseberry's tailor to stitch him amongst other clothes a pair of breeches that was a combination of riding trousers and the churidar. Compared to other breeches, this new pair had an extra length with a cuff that nestled on top of low riding boots. It came to be known as Jodhpur breeches.

True to its unisex origins, women in Europe too adopted the Jodhpur breeches. It freed them from riding horse's side-saddle. The longer length and extra width around the thighs allowed for a freedom of movement. Chanel, Marni, Jean-Paul Gautier and Miu Miu, have all created their own versions of churidars as breeches or skinny trousers. Its popularity is always high because it highlights the best part of the leg, which is the calves, and camouflages the tricky parts like the thighs. It is beautiful, sexy and wearable by all ages and sexes; as an undergarment, as a riding outfit, or just as it is.

CHYAWANPRASH

A modern health supplement prepared with an ancient recipe

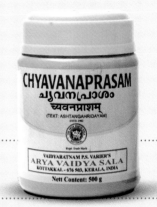

Date of Origin: Around 1 CE
Material: Indian gooseberry, honey, raisins, ghee, sandalwood

Lifestyle drugs and health foods are coming of age now internationally but they have for a long time been an obsession in India. Chyawanprash is the commercial name of a 2000-year-old elixir made of emblica officinalis or Indian gooseberry and forty-nine other ingredients. First mentioned in the *Charak Samhita*, a guide to Ayurveda from the fourth century BC, regularly consuming chyawanprash is believed to increase life span by improving digestion and immunity. The philosophy behind the design of these elixirs is sophisticated as they aim to create an optimum balance between the human body and its surrounding environment.

Indian philosophy equates health with wealth. According to the *Atharva Veda*, an eighth-century treatise on metallurgy and alchemy, the value of longevity of life is physically measurable to the weight of gold. So while the thirty chapters of Charaka Samhita are cures to various ailments, its most important chapter called the 'Rasayana' is solely dedicated to the pharmaceutics of longevity and vitality, a branch of medical science that has come of age globally only very recently.

Rasa refers to the six tastes – sweet, sour, saline, astringent, bitter, and pungent. This combination affects the palate, and thus health. Rasa also refers to the plasma or the tissue that makes up the human body and Rasayana is the path that this primary tissue takes in the body. Multiple combinations of the six basic rasas in turn produce sixty-three rasas that form the properties of all foods and medicines. Amongst them those rasas that enhance both physical and mental strength and promote youth, health and beauty are rated as the rasa for Rasayana. For perfect balance, Rasayana formulations are prepared from a combination of three categories – animal products like honey, milk, horns, hoofs and nails; herbs and plants; and products derived from the earth such as gold, lime and gems.

The consumption of elixirs daily is unique to India, a practice that has been carried down to contemporary life through Chyawanprash, a modern health food that is available at millions of stores nationwide. Some components of the packaging designed in the 1970s are still in use today. At that time there was a need to package traditional elixirs into a more modern homogenized format meant for mass retail. So while a standardized plastic container was used to evoke modernity, its label had a sage and its key ingredient, the Indian gooseberry or amla, as a reminder of its historic formulation taken from the Rasayana in the 1940s. Apart from the Indian gooseberry it contains honey, raisins and sandalwood, but every home has its own recipe including modern age ones using almonds, sugar, and spices. Whatever the recipe, generations of Indians have grown up consuming this modern elixir and have placed their trust in it to help combat everything from common cold and acne to wrinkles.

CYCLE RICKSHAW
Mainstay of transport, a three-wheeled cycle with a seat

Date of Origin: Around 1880, Shimla
Material: Metal, rubber, plastic

By 1914, the Chinese in India were using rickshaws to pull transport goods from warehouses to shops and shortly afterwards it became a convenient transportation for passengers, first on the hilly roads of Shimla and then in the bustling port city of Calcutta. Within three decades the cycle rickshaws started plying on the streets all over the country. The addition of the bicycle to the seat was an improvement from the hand-pulled earlier ones. Incidentally, both had come in with the immigrant Chinese. The use of rickshaws proliferated to many cities around the country because it was a cheap means of transport and there was a steady supply of indigent workers for whom it was the only source of employment in the city.

The most common use for rickshaws was ferrying children to and from school. For this, a small wooden bench was added between the seat of the person pedalling and the main seat where school bags and water bottles could be hung. Rickshaws were typically divided into two parts: the front bicycle handle frame and the peddler's seat, and the back which is a long seat structure supported by the chassis. Essentially the rickshaw is a structurally strengthened bicycle. While strong enough to carry the weight, it was also heavy and difficult to peddle.

The basic design of the rickshaw had remained unchanged till about late-1990s. The model was called the 'Meerut body' and had a foldable hood, narrow front and back seating with very little back support and a relatively high step-up. The body frame was made of iron, the seat cushion of coir, and the hood frame was joined with an accordion in plastic on strips of wood. In a country where people love to express their individuality, the rickshaw-pullers chose rickshaws in bright colours and even gave them names. They were customised with decorations such as false pleated hair (*parandas*), plastic flowers, and to ward off the evil eye, a chilli and lemon.

Due to the arrival of the Maruti 800 car in 1980s, the number of rickshaws began to diminish in cities. But at the end of the 1990s as roads started choking with motorized traffic and the awareness of environmental pollution grew, the government decided to try to resuscitate interest in cycle rickshaws. This led to the launch of a new design in 2001. The rickshaws were made lighter; a new metal frame brought the original weight of 150 down by ten to fifteen kilogrammes. The floor was lowered so that it was easier for passengers to step up; the passenger seat was given a high back; and the narrow back seat got a safety handle with wider seats. The accordion-style canopy was replaced with a permanent one.

These changes make passengers willing to ride more often and also travel longer distances, which in turn means that the pullers' incomes doubled. Today, around three hundred thousand of these modern rickshaws ply streets in nine cities; while providing a livelihood, they also help keep the environment 'green'.

DABBA

These stacked boxes are used to carry millions of meals daily from homes to offices

Date of Origin: 1890, Bombay
Material: Stainless steel, aluminium

From the Japanese bento box to the Chinese takeaway or the baguette sandwich clutched in a Frenchman's hand, every nation has figured a smart way to carry food. India's response to this is the simple dabba, or the 'tiffin carrier', that in Bombay is hand-delivered to office everyday by the dabbawala. Its humble design but unassailable supply chain management is as efficient as DHL – the difference being computers and trucks are replaced with a simple coding system and basic public transport.

The dabba is a stackable box container full of the nation's favourite power lunch placed in separate boxes before being conveniently strapped together by a metal frame with a clip and a carrier handle. It is unknown how this particular stacked design originated in India. But its widespread popularity is because its separation is perfect for carrying different textures, from solid to liquid without mixing. More recent designs are made of plastic, but earlier ones were made of brass, and the most popular ones are of aluminium and stainless steel because these metals keep the food warm.

Dabba delivery first began in the 1890s to help Bombay, a mercantile city, eat freshly prepared home-cooked meal delivered at workplace. Churchgate, the city's historic station, teems with dabbawala men sorting and hand-delivering lunches or 'tiffins' on a simple pushcart to offices and schools throughout the city.

Within an hour starting 9:30 a.m, the dabbas are picked up from homes and taken to the nearest station. Three hours later, after journeying with passengers through an extremely busy city, the dabbas arrive at the destination station where they are sorted and delivered to the respective customers. For accurate delivery, they use markers with a coding system to identify the area, building, floor and office, much like the postman with the pincode, but faster and surer. After lunch, these are then collected again at 2:30 p.m. and sorted and delivered back to the homes between 3:30 to 5 p.m. The ritual is repeated with clockwork precision on every working day of the year and despite its complexity, an error occurs in the dabbawala system only once every six million deliveries.

At a very affordable two hundred rupees a month, this service has a hundred and seventy-five thousand takers. The investment required from these simple dabbawalas is only precision and timekeeping. As a public station space is used for sorting the thousands of dabbas, Churchgate has a paparazzi of tourists snapping this busy site, but most importantly, the Bombaywala nourishes himself from it. Flood or shine, the dabbawala is a constant every single working day of the year. And in ensuring delivery such that a dabba is never disposed off after use, he sets a template for designing and consuming fresh food.

DATUN

The ancient practice of using neem for oral care

Date of Origin: 800 CE
Material: Neem twig

The toothbrush was introduced to India only in the early nineteenth century. Until then a small twig plucked everyday from the Azadirachta Indica tree, also known as the Margosatree, or Neem, had defined oral hygiene in the country for centuries. When rubbed against the teeth it served as both toothpaste and toothbrush. Not any branch but only a young teig with a thin skin of the Neem tree is used for a datun. The fibres separate when used, so is used only once, and after use it is bent and becomes a tongue cleaner.

According to Indian mythology, when amrit or the elixir of immortality was being carried to heaven, it dropped on Neem, imbuing every single part of the tree with curative properties. The use of every single part of the Neem tree, from its leaves, bark and twigs to its roots in external, internal and surgical medicine have been well documented in the Ayurvedic guides *Charak Samhita* and *Susruta Samhita*. The twig is beneficial to cure cough, asthma and diabetes, the leaf helps with eye and skin disorders, the bark with fever, and the fruit for digestive problems.

For 2,000 years this wisdom was intact but without any scientific proof. In 1942, S. Siddiqui, a scientist, isolated the first active compound from Neem oil called nimbin. Since then over a hundred compounds of Neem have been isolated, the most active being *nimbid*, which is useful as an anti-inflammatory, anti-fungal and anti-bacterial ingredient. The simple twigs were then transformed into modern toothpastes and mouthwashes with Neem compounds. Tests confirmed that neem cures caries and inhibits bacteria that cause tooth decay.

Siddiqui's research triggered an interest amongst many other researchers who carefully analyzed and confirmed thousands of years of Indian belief. So until toothpastes arrived to do the actual cleaning of the teeth with modern abrasives, the datun preserved the health of not just the gums but also the body. Meanwhile in India, the ancient Grand Trunk routes that form the highways of western India are now dotted with neem trees, it is hard to tell that this was a desert until the 1950s. While the tree had many therapeutic uses, it could also grow in hot climates without much water. These trees were therefore planted just after Independence to stop the creeping expansion of the desert. This is not a coincidence – as in Hindu belief, planting three or more neem trees is considered to be a path to heaven!

DESERT COOLER
A home-made air conditioner

Date of Origin: 1950s
Material: Straw, metal

In the eighteenth century, people in India cooled spaces during hot summer months with a humid woven grass or textile filter positioned between the hot air outside and the room inside. A manually-operated fan placed behind the grass curtain pushed hot air through the moisture-laden filter, cooling down the room considerably. In the 1950s this led to the ingenious creation of the 'desert cooler'. Unlike its predecessor, the fan ran on electricity and was incorporated in a box. The use of water for cooling is ideally suited for desert conditions of dry heat with little or no humidity. It is environment-friendly and cost-effective as it is one-fourth the price of an air conditioner and its running cost is just one-tenth.

The desert cooler was a simple evolution using the electricians' ingenuity and the tradition of wet chiks during summer. A fan was covered with a box that was lined with grass. To make the cooler, three parts – an exhaust fan, a water pump and two water tanks – are fitted in a metal cube structure. The front panel has the fan and the three other panels (the rear and the two other sides) are open and lined with vetiver-scented dried grass. The water tanks are at the top and bottom. The upper tank has three rows of holes on three sides so that water from the tank drips down, wets the grass on the three panels and collects in the tank at the bottom. An electric pump circulates the water from the bottom tank back up to the upper tank ensuring

that the water keeps flowing through and over the grass mesh.

The fan facing front, along with the whole air cooler structure behind, is fitted on the window of the room so that the dry air can only enter the room by passing through the wet grass mesh capturing the moisture and thus evaporating the water. This evaporation needs heat which it takes from the air as well as the remaining water. Thus the air getting into the room is gradually cooler, as is the water collecting at the bottom of the tank. The process is repeated as this cool water is pumped and the room becomes cooler gradually. For those who understood the cooler's mechanism, it became the first object often made in a 'DIY' (do-it-yourself) style as all its parts could be easily sourced from the local hardware store. Initially the object looked more like a 'contraption' sticking out of the window. Branded coolers came in not because they were better but they were more attractive aesthetically, compared to the electrician and carpenter's hand job.

In dry conditions the evaporation rate is higher and the cooler is as effective as an air conditioner. In a humid climate, however, evaporation is low and the cooler makes the air more sultry, making the machine unsuitable for monsoons. Until air conditioning came in, this was India's clever way of ensuring a good night's sleep in hot summer months.

DHOBI ISTRI
An indigenous version of the steam iron

Date of Origin: 1900 CE
Material: Metal, coal

When the daughter of a dhobi marries, her dowry contains very little – only a few necessities, and an iron. This iron, also called 'istri' or 'press', is different from modern irons. In reality it is a metal plate with a charcoal chamber built on top of it. The charcoal iron's uniqueness lies in its form. Made from metal, traditionally iron or brass, it has a hollow interior that can be filled with hot coals. The top is hinged and has a removable metal plate for filling coal. To keep the coals burning, it has holes for air and a vent for smoke. The handle made of wood insulates the hand from the heat of the coals. Its unique form makes it portable and not dependent on electricity, the reason why it is still so popular in India.

The dhobis were a nomadic community with the traditional occupation of washing clothes, who with time evolved into a caste. The village of Kayalapadu in Andhra Pradesh, for example, is made up almost entirely of members of this dhobi caste. But as all of India needs ironed clothes, dhobis have migrated all over the country. With their portable press, they set up temporary sheds on the street in neighbourhoods where they usually have a small open kiln where coal is burnt.

The standard press is made of cast iron, while the really prized ones are made of brass. New ones come in over a dozen sizes: the smaller ones are meant for the home where electric irons are actually preferred, and the larger ones for the dhobi community. As weight contributes to heat on a well-ironed garment, the largest ones still weigh more than eight kilogrammes when filled with charcoal, and have a stocky hardwood grip that helps the dhobi hold the iron tight. They are extremely durable as many dhobis use the same iron for over twenty to thirty years.

Dhobis work area-wise. Their daily work involves collecting dirty clothes from twenty or thirty homes. The clothes are then taken to a dhobi ghat, for washing and drying following which they are ironed back in the house or neighbourhood workspace. Over time, the dhobis migrated to other countries like Kuwait, Singapore, Malaysia and South Africa where they maintained their occupation and continued to be referred to locally as 'dhobis'. In fact, the Dhoby Ghaut area in Singapore has been named after a dhobi's place of work.

The dhobis quickly adapted to the widespread availability of electricity, setting up automated laundry and ironing facilities in neighbourhood shopping centres. In Bur Dubai, the centre of the Indian community in Dubai, the tradition of the dhobi is well preserved. At around the same time each day, the dhobi cycles up to the large apartment blocks constructed on the desert sand. He parks his bicycle, rides up the elevator and knocks on every door, collecting bundles of clothes before returning to his laundry, washing and ironing the clothes neatly, and returning them the next day. And so the tradition continues.

DHOTI / LUNGI

A single piece of cloth draped over the lower part of the body

Date of Origin: Around 1–3 CE
Material: Cotton, silk, linen

The beauty of the dhoti lies in its drape, the most effective form of clothing as it can be simply wrapped around the body in a protective sheath. The palm-leaf-like fan created by the pleats of the dhoti in the front give it character and style, turning it into an article of clothing. An unstitched dhoti is considered the purest form of dress and therefore appropriate for wearing at religious ceremonies. To wear it, four and a half metres of cloth – often white when in cotton, or beige when in silk – is tied around the waist in a knot. The remaining piece is then pleated and tucked into the waist from front and at the back, thus draping it elegantly around the legs.

Lungis too are a form of draping, and their comfort, versatility and ease of wear makes them very popular, perhaps even more than the dhoti. Lungis come in two simple varieties – stitched and unstitched. The former is pulled over the head and tied in a pretzel-like knot on the side. The latter is simply hitched up and tucked in at the waist. When part of work attire, lungis are folded at the knee or above, otherwise they stay full length.

When the cartoonist R.K. Laxman created the 'common man', the longest running cartoon in India, he gave it the wardrobe of the dhoti with a coat because a balding man in a dhoti-coat was for Laxman a representation of the omnipresent everybody. Mahatma Gandhi too adopted the dhoti with a casually draped shawl as his daily wardrobe. In fact he created a variant wearing a shorter dhoti that stopped at the knees. This indigenous khadi dhoti would compete in price with the full-length dhoti imported from Manchester.

The Chennai-based VSG Lungi Company, India's largest maker of lungis and owner of Nandu or 'crab' brand of lungis, sells 30,000 lungis every day to the poorest and the richest of clients. For farmers and fishermen they are work-wear, and for politicians, particularly in south India, they replace the 'power suit'.

In Kerala, where lungis are practically de rigueur, most lungis are white, but gradually the fashion changed and they now come in all colours. Checks and stripes are the most common patterns and every season sees innumerable new designs. Black, however, is rarely worn. This could be because of the humid and hot weather in Kerala or because it is an inauspicious colour.

In the film *Chennai Express*, filmstar Shahrukh Khan dons a lungi with a tuxedo jacket in a dance sequence, where the song is also named after the garment.

Both the dhoti and the lungi were the most common lower garments worn by men and women for centuries until the nineteenth century when work demanded more 'cosmopolitan' clothing, and both the dhoti and the lungi became relegated to just lounge or ceremonial wear. But it's the women who have brought innovation, the dhoti being worn as a salwar – dhoti salwars or pants are stitched with pleating inside the leg. This gives both volume and presence to the silhouette making the kurta look contemporary. While national costumes around the world disappear, the dhoti maintains its ancient form by keeping it relevant to the times.

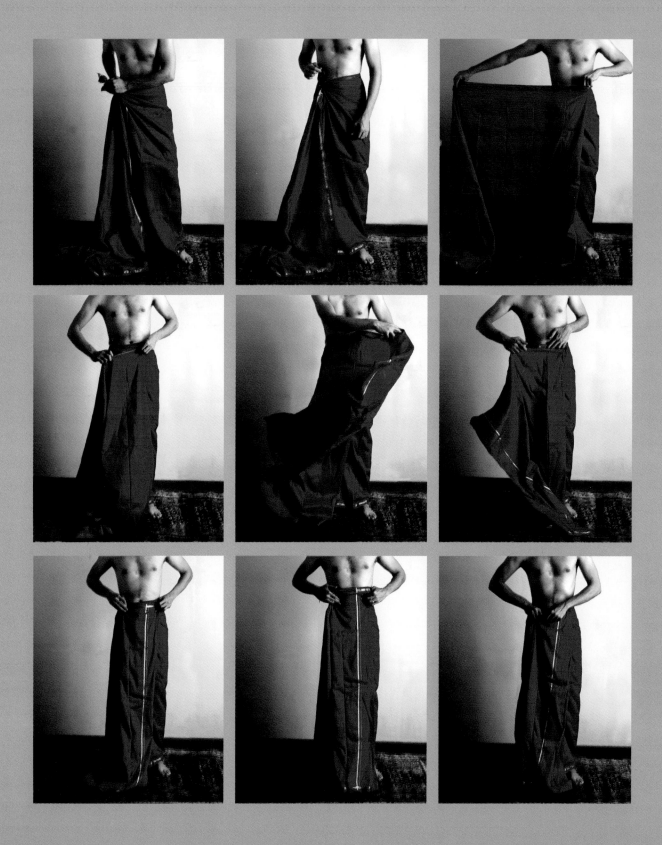

DHURRIE

Floor coverings in a range of virtuoso colours, graphics and sizes

Date of Origin: 200 BCE
Material: Cotton, wool, jute

The world discovered the dhurrie at the 1851 Crystal Palace exhibition in London; but in fact it originated in India and is the world's oldest floor covering, with a long history of its own. The word was first used in English in 1880, borrowed from the Hindi and Urdu word darī, which means carpet.

The tradition of pile carpets came to India in the sixteenth century through Persian pile carpet makers who were on the Mughal King Akbar's payroll. They created the tradition of Indian pile carpets that borrowed from Iran in using a similar knot but rivalling it in its sumptuousness of decoration. At that time, dhurries were woven with the simplest of designs and had a far more functional role than the luxurious pile carpets, primarily used on large floors.

In the eighteenth century, the most common of these were also used in homes and known as the Satarangis, decorated with stripes, often blue, red or white. Dhurries were preferred also because the relentless heat prevented the use of thick carpets, as in Europe. Thus the eighteenth century saw a revival of the dhurries in jails, where inmates produced from coarse and simple dhurries to the most magnificent pieces. These created a genre called the 'jail dhurries' or pictorial dhurries that used a combination of geometric motifs such as lozenges along with natural motifs like birds. These jail dhurries are still being produced both in jails and commercially.

Indian dhurries have a balance and a unique harmony as shades were cleverly blended into one another without clear breaks, or were there clear breaks? Dhurrie weavers do not follow measured patterns when translating the design into weaves. A conductor recites the pattern from paper vocally to the weavers in a rhythmic way and the weavers translate this into design by ear. It is as if someone tells the weavers what the design should look like and they often interpret it without a drawing.

Due to their popularity after the 1851 exhibition, UK-based carpet manufacturers opened facilities in India and started giving commissions to Indian weavers for dhurrie designs that would sell in Europe. For example, the introduction of a new colour palette based on primary colours with clear breaks rather than shades that blended into each other, which was an Indian practice. This led to a confusion of design patterns and thus instituted the decline of rug-weaving until much later in the 1980s when Shyam Ahuja, India's biggest proponent of dhurries, decided to revive the industry by making classic motifs contemporary and relevant within and outside India.

Today there is a rich mix of designs, between traditional Indian, English and even French Savonnerie and Aubusson. Thus the rhythm woven by the weavers, combined with the dhurrie's roots in India's idyllic rural landscape, and an afterlife as an international floor showpiece has made every dhurrie unique, modern and classic.

DUPATTA
A multi-purpose stole

Date of Origin: 1500–1100 BCE
Material: Silk, cotton, chiffon

The dupatta was initially worn over the sari. The epic poem *Padmavat*, written (by Malik Muhammad Jayasi) in 1540 CE, recounts how women wore a sari knotted around the waist or cinched with a girdle. A veil covered the top of the body often draped loosely around the shoulders. The beauty of the drape was in the fineness of the cloth, of which there were many anecdotes. Amir Khusro says that when folded it was the size of a fingernail and when open it could wrap the whole world.[9] But dupattas or garments were worn much earlier and can be seen in the cave paintings of Ajanta.

The development of the dupatta does not lie with the salwar kameez but with the sari. By the fourteenth century, the one-piece garment that women had worn for centuries was unfortunately considered too scanty and revealing, so it was first cut up into two, the top and the bottom, following which the bottom was no longer made of fine muslin, but a thicker fabric to cover the legs and called the lehenga. The diaphanous veil stayed on the top of the body and was called the *odhni*, another name for the dupatta that has stayed till date. Fifteenth-century paintings from Gujarat show contemporary women's wear of that time.

Since then the dupatta, as its name suggests, became part of the two-piece wear that all women adapted, particularly in the northern part of the country. Its sheer beauty and existence in various colours, materials and embroidery depending on the region has meant that throughout Indian history, this piece of garment has been venerated by poets. By the sixteenth century, during the reigns of the Mughals, the salwar–kameez was introduced under the dupatta and has stayed current. The dupatta came in varying lengths varying from just over 2 metres worn loosely over both the shoulders to three or even four metres worn tucked into the waist, through the legs almost sari like and thrown over the shoulders. Under the stewardship of Mahatma Gandhi and Jawaharlal Nehru, in the spirit of national unity, the dupatta travelled the nation and was slowly adopted as common daily wear particularly among young women. In time the dupatta, this seemingly 'formalist' attire could not escape fashion's critical gaze. The length was shortened and it was lovingly draped just over one shoulder. Today this versatile garment stays perched on a woman's shoulder as much about adornment as it is about subtle empowerment.

GAMCHA
A thin multi-purpose towel

Date of Origin: Unknown
Material: Cotton, muslin

Gamchas are the Indian version of handkerchiefs. A gamcha is probably the most humble piece of clothing in the country, but it is also the most versatile– it is even used for catching fish and making *mishti doi*! It originates from the Prakrit word 'angoccha' or scarf, a piece of cloth considered respectable male clothing. It can be worn slung loosely on one shoulder, scarf-like or tied on the head as a turban. In this role it is particularly welcomed by working men in the hot humid weather, for its hand-spun and hand-woven texture is porous and dries quicker than the thicker toweling material; a boon in the rainy months.

Their graphic presence is singular in a sea of utilitarian garments. Gamchas have always been made of cotton gingham checks or 'Madras checks'. The designer Gaurav Gupta finds this a thoroughly modern approach for such an ancient garment, a peppy look for a garment that could easily be relegated when it came to design.

Wearing a gamcha often reflects a certain economic affiliation as mostly workers wear it, almost as a proud sign of their social status. For labourers on construction sites this is their uniform. Station coolies use it as padding on their heads to rest heavy luggage. Fishermen in Assam and West Bengal use gamchas made of muslin. For them gamchas are not just articles of clothing. They are used to catch spawn in the shallow end of river waters. They make a shooting net called Benchijal from this cloth. It is a tube with two round openings of different diameters. When slung across sticks in the river, it helps catch carp eggs that flow in from one side and are caught at the bottom. The spawn that hatches is collected from the gamcha a day later.

In the same part of the country, gamchas have another ingenious usage – muslin gamchas are used in the kitchen as strainers for mishti doi. A mix of caramelized sugar and buffalo milk yoghurt are strained to separate the water and gather paste to make a rich dessert. But women too have been wearing a gamcha since the Vedic period. It is in a longer version called the dupatta. It is utilitarian like the gamchas for men, but more than that, dupattas are part of the elegance and chutzpah of a woman's daily dress.

GHUNGROO

An anklet that provides rhythm

Date of Origin: 500 BCE–500 CE
Material: Brass bells, leather, cotton string

The unique thing about the ghungroo is that it was designed purely for its sound, and is hence reserved for dance. These bells on ankles are not just for women but men and boys too. This unisex dancer's accessory looks equally comely on both a man and a woman, and becomes the heart of every beat of the foot; what would have otherwise been just a flat thump on the floor is transformed into a reverberating melody.

Its archetype is the rope, in the form of a ring – a shape important to Indian jewellery that could be adapted for the finger, arms, waist, and ankles. At its simplest, it could even be a chord with bells. It is in the *Natyashastra* or the 'science of dance' that there is clear reference to anklets as ornaments, giving them the same status as clothes, or articles that are meant to be worn by all dancers, men and women. In fact Siva, also known as Lord Nataraja, in his dancing form wears a pair of anklets. Ghungroos are also used as accompanying instruments to provide rhythm while dancing.

In its simplest initial version, the anklet was just a large metal ring. They became more elaborate as chains or tubes in varying thicknesses depending on the region, style and occasion. In southern India this is called a *toda* and is made by lacing several silver or gold wires into a coil that rests around the ankle. When bells are attached to them for sound, they adopt onomatopoeic names like *kinkini* and *jhanjhan*. In fact kinkini could also refer to the sound from the waist. The bells are set on bands made variously of velvet cloth, leather or simply cotton chord. Traditionally, women layered the ghungroo with a payal. The payal, an evolution from the ring anklet, was a specific kind of anklet with chains that were flexible. It is the ancient Sanskrit text *Manasollasa* that gives the first reference to the payal, as five or more chains attached together at equal intervals that could sometimes be studded with precious stones.

Anklets, also called *nupura*, amongst all jewellery were the ones that were often taken on and off, or could just slip off and leave a trace of its wearer. Valimiki gives an account of this in the Ramayana – Sita let her anklets fall on the ground when Ravana kidnapped her. Later Rama traces her to the point where he found her anklets, an important landmark in his search for her. Valmiki describes the sound of anklets as kūjita, cocooing or jingling. The delicate sound of the payal and the ghungroo is to evoke pleasure not just in the wearer but also in those around.

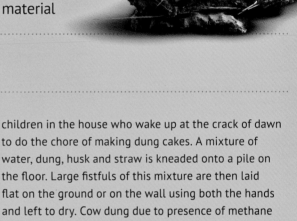

GOBAR UPLA

Cow dung cakes used as fuel as well as building material

Date of Origin: 5500 BCE, Mehrgarh
Material: Cow dung

Even though it's free, widely available and the cost of production is negligible, cow dung is probably the most undervalued design material in the world. Except in India, where cow dung is used for many things – from making houses and toys to what is perhaps one of its biggest uses: fuel and even electricity. As livestock manure is available the world over, this centuries old fuel from India is slowly being embraced worldwide.

Most Hindus believe that the cow is sacred but few know exactly why. In fact, the word 'gau' (commonly referred to the cow) signifies the first ray of the sun that falls on the plants, which also serves as a fertilizer, causing the sap to rise. It is this movement of birth, growth and death that is revered in Hindu philosophy. Cows are a symbol of this cycle of energy and almost everything it provides has a use. Its milk is drunk, its urine is used as medicine, its horns are used for making objects, and cow dung is used as fuel and fertilizer.

Cow dung is collected in bamboo baskets from pastures where the cattle graze. Sometimes it's the children in the house who wake up at the crack of dawn to do the chore of making dung cakes. A mixture of water, dung, husk and straw is kneaded onto a pile on the floor. Large fistfuls of this mixture are then laid flat on the ground or on the wall using both the hands and left to dry. Cow dung due to presence of methane is a source of 'free' energy, a fuel for cooking, and a pesticide. The cow dung is also used as a slurry wash on the mud floor and external walls of houses in villages. It serves as an efficient mortar that fixes the underlying structure into shape.

It is hard to say what came first, the enthroning of the cow as India's sacred animal par excellence or the widespread use of cow dung as a fuel and a natural pesticide. But ancient Indian texts from the Vedic period record the use of cow dung and urine in the manufacture of medicine and organic pesticides. Today, the International Energy Agency states that fuel from cow dung and other such biomasses can remove the pressure off fossil fuels by meeting one fourth of the world's fuel needs.

GODREJ ALMIRAH

The steel almirah is the most trusted vault of the nation

Date of Origin: 1920
Material: Steel

For over a century, most of India has secured precious mementos and priceless heirlooms in the Godrej steel almirah. It was retailed at just Rs 180 in 1920 and has since been the trusted vault of the nation. The reason for its popularity is that the Godrej almirah is basically an oversized safe with a very strong lock.

In July 1908, Ardeshir Godrej invented and patented a lever lock without springs. Locks until then used springs that were prone to rusting resulting in the failure of the lock mechanism. Ardeshir also invented a new safe design that, contrary to the current designs that existed in Europe, could not be dismantled into pieces. Amongst the many innovations he made to the body of the safe, one of the most important one was that the locking mechanism was attached to the inner steel sheet of a double plate door, thus out of reach of theft. The Godrej almirah was thus born. It was a combination of reinforced plate doors and unpickable locks, and was hence named Godrej Patent Safe Cabinets.

Prominent in every home, and present in every government office, the almirah has always symbolized security from both theft and dust. The first models were similar to the ones currently in use. They are reinforced with bolts secured by a lock doubly protected by a steel plate and finished in grey enamel. Their spacious design – a double door almost two metres high, half a metre wide and comfortably deep, was perfect for safe storage.

Godrej's reincarnation of the wooden cabinet was widely popular for its affordability, invincibility and good design with a lustrous finish yet utilitarian appeal. Despite an industrial look and mechanical feel, by the late 1960s the Godrej almirah was being used in homes as well. It even became an important part of the wedding trousseau with a special space for storing the bride's numerous saris, wedding jewellery, and other keepsakes.

Before product placement became commonplace in the media, this almirah debuted in Bollywood films as the prototypical family emblem. In reality, a family's affluence was equal to the rows of locked almirahs and metallic trunks that stood as sentinels to their wealth in the 'box room', a room in the house that served as both storage and vault. For those with a smaller square footage, the Godrej almirah took pride of place in the bedroom or the balcony. A classic wooden almirah evokes nostalgia but Godrej's steel almirah remains an asset in every Indian's abode.

GODREJ TYPEWRITER

The first multi-lingual typewriter of the world

Date of Origin: 1955
Material: Rubber, metal, plastic

Typewriters are engineering marvels as they are made of more than two thousand parts and the manufacturing of each part requires putting in place specific machine tools. The Godrej typewriter was the first ever manual typewriter made in Asia and was referred to as the 'all-Indian typewriter'. To make a typewriter is itself a feat, but Godrej went a step further and introduced keyboards in multiple languages, something unheard of at that time. Introduced in 1955, the keyboard was equipped with English and mathematical symbols, and also Hindi, Marathi, Gujarati, Tamil, Telugu, and Kannada. Over the years there has not been any radical change in the typewriter – a hard typeface that imprints through an ink-ribbon – but for the addition of electric keys and memory. Providing a vast variety of keyboards made the design difficult, which Godrej, a company with no experience in the design of typewriters, pulled off ingeniously.

The development of this typewriter was spurred by the call for swaraj or self-rule and indigenous manufacturing capacity. In the newly independent India of the 1950s, the demand for typewriters was very limited with less than 8,000 typewriters in use. The new typewriter was in competition with imported brands like Remington, Olivetti, Underwood, and an Indian typewriter called Halda. So, three engineers from Godrej – KNV Vasan, PM Bhada and KB Gupte – formed a small design team at the Godrej facilities in Lalbag, Bombay. They meticulously ripped and studied different models and designs such as the American typewriter Woodstock's 1947 model. The final version, christened Godrej AB after the founder of Godrej, had a wide fourteen-inch carriage with a key added on the front for tab stops. Apart from the Indian languages, Godrej made keyboards for Thai and Russian, and special typewriters with right to left carriage movement for Arabic, Urdu and Persian.

All the 1,800 components of the typewriter were indigenous, including 150 varieties of screws and threads, and specialized machines such as the multi-spindle drilling machines for mounting the key levers; only the types, key tops, rubber plates and one spring were imported. The resulting typewriter had 2,220 parts and came in two conservative colours brown and green. It went on sale for Rs 630. Between 1965 and 1970, 24,258 machines found their place in the market – the typewriter revolutionized communication in all parts of the country.

In thirty years Godrej launched five models, and became a leader in manual machines with Godrej Prima, introduced in 1983, because it was easy to use and punching was soft. While the Godrej design team was struggling, typing became a national hobby for all those who could buy a typewriter. Between 1982 and 1994, 2,92,000 typists participated in National Speed Typing championships, gathering publicity and recognition for themselves as typists.

Today, even though Godrej created electronic typewriters, manual typewriters are still in demand in thirteen Indian languages and some international ones like Russian, Polish, French, Czech, Arabic and Persian – not out of nostalgia but because they force the writer to be exacting, make no mistakes and be disciplined: the hallmarks of a great typist.

GULABPASH

A rose water sprinkler for all auspicious occasions

Date of Origin: 1600 CE
Material: Silver, enamel, gilt

A gulabpash is a rose water sprinkler that takes the art of welcoming guests to a refined extreme. Hand-held and sprinkled above the heads of arriving guests, especially during weddings, it showers them with fragrant rose water. Everyone knows this but what few know is that the rose water sprinkler is also used in the confines of one's home on oneself as a gesture of purification after being in the presence of something or someone undesirable. It's a way of protecting oneself from a collision of ideas.

The form was created in India and has always shown unusual grace. Often made of silver, the body of the sprinkler that also serves as its base is always oval in shape with a neck and a top. Though it is designed as one solid piece, the bottom can be unscrewed to pour rose water in and then screwed back on to the top. A typical gulabpash is often between ten to eleven inches in height.

The gulabpash was part of courtly material culture starting from the seventeenth century (along with paan dans) and great attention was paid to their design. They could be silver cast, engraved, enamelled, gilt and chased or made of glass with gilt decoration. They were treasured possessions and often designed by the best artisans in India, such as silversmiths in Hyderabad and Lucknow or later even at glassmakers in London (because in the late eighteenth century, British-made glass was considered superior to glass made in India).

India has many varieties of roses that have since centuries been extracted as absolutes, which is extraction of smell from petals by laying them on fat or grease. Rose water is not an absolute, it is an essential oil. It is unknown when it was first used but the story goes that a Rajasthani princess discovered fragrant smelling foam in her hot bath of rose petals. So even though the know-how of extraction of petals as an absolute was well known for centuries, its steam distillation was discovered by a happy accident. No other natural fragrance has a purpose-built diffuser, which is where the gulabpash takes its name from.

In today's India, life carries on without the gulabpash. But its spirit of elevation stays. In its use whether as a ritual to welcome guests or on oneself, it is a product of the constant striving to do things better – to make an object that is not only efficient but beautiful, and through this object to turn a mundane ritual into an expression of great honour.

HINDUSTAN AMBASSADOR

India's first car

Date of Origin: 1958
Material: Metal, rubber, plastic

At the 2002 Auto Expo in New Delhi, 20,000 Indians defined the Ambassador's greatest attribute as its 'emotional connect'. With its wide grill and round headlights, it was easily the most recognizable car on the road. The initial model, based on the 1948 Morris Oxford Series II, had an egg-shell shaped structural skin with a rounded rear and a dimpled sloping hood. Initial versions had bench seats in the front and back with instrumentation panels in the dashboard's centre and a gear stick on the steering wheel bar. While the latter made the car difficult to drive, its springy, spacious seats, which happily incorporated an entire family, or two, made the car a beast of burden.

Manufactured by Hindustan Motors, it was the first indigenously-produced car to hit the roads in 1957. At that time the Indian government had banned the import of cars. So the Ambassador acquired supremacy over Indian roads at a time when socialist India was starved of cars. The first elections in independent India concluded in 1952. The government ordered and continued to order close to one-fourth of the company's production. There were only three models available until the Japanese came in with the urbane 800cc Maruti Suzuki in 1983. So for over three decades it was only the 'Amby' that was the preferred mode of transport for all those who could afford a car, as it was considered to be both efficient and an all-terrain vehicle. Such was its popularity that till 2002 it included amongst its users the prime minister of India.

Politicians and bureaucrats were using it to travel to semi-urban areas till very recently.

All through the 1960s and 1970s the Ambassador managed to stay unchanged with only minor changes in the models. But as legislation tightened its grip on the auto industry, the Ambassador 1800 ISZ was released with an environment-friendly engine. This change demanded that bench seats become bucket seats, so the dashboard changed and seatbelts were added along with other modern upgrades like power steering. However, with liberalization many international carmakers entered the country in the 1990s – in the heydays of the Ambassador's popularity, India boasted only three car manufacturers, but now there were over thirty. After four decades of rule over the Indian roads, this influx of newer, cheaper cars has substantially dented the Amby's popularity, but not quite ended it, as 33,000 Ambassador taxis in Calcutta alone continue to ply. To its users the car does not represent technology but familiarity, safety and roominess.

In May 2014, the production of India's first car stopped after seventy-one years of history. The late photographer Raghubir Singh dedicated an important part of his last major body of work 'A Way into India' (1999) to the Ambassador car. For over thirty years he took photographs of the car in various everyday roles – from a transport for chickens, a taxi ferrying tourists to the Red Fort, to a family car with at least three generations inside it – using it as the car that framed India's tryst with modernity.

HOOKAH

A centuries-old tobacco-smoking equipment

Date of Origin: 1500 CE
Material: Metal, glass, leather, cotton

It is believed that the hookah originated in India in the sixteenth century. One of the physicians in the court of the Mughal emperor Akbar, Irfan Sheikh, is attributed to having invented it. It's from here that the use of the hookah spread far and wide through Persia and into North Africa. All hookah-smoking countries have their own designs but Indian hookahs have a particularly rich and diverse material heritage. Miniature paintings, particularly in the eighteenth century, portray the exchange between the notables, aristocrats and kings while sharing a hookah.

A hookah has three sections: a base that contains water and includes the stand on which it rests on, a container or cup for charcoal and flavoured tobacco on the top, and single or more long pipes with a mouthpiece at the end that is used to smoke it. The pleasure of smoking the hookah is enhanced by the high water content of the smoke.

Hookahs were designed to be shared. They were passed around amongst guests while information was being exchanged. This led to the innovation of a specific seating pattern. The hookah was smoked seated on the floor in a posture where the back was straight. The need to make this position comfortable gave rise to a unique form of cushion called *musnud*. The seat was also padded and called a *gaddi*. They were elevated a few inches off the ground and were surrounded by a low wooden support. This sitting style was completed with a canopy on gilt pillars. Hookahs were an integral part of this set-up that became representative of power. (In fact, the word *gaddi* also means a seat of power.) While other items of aristocratic pleasure like pan daan, etc., were exquisite objects of desire, the hookah was different because it had an important role in power play.

Hookahs were an integral part of all courts. Each of the three parts was designed as luxurious objects: the base was sometimes of jade inlaid with turquoise; its body could be of jade or gold-plated silver. As mouth pieces were the closest to the body, even more attention was paid to them. In the seventeenth century, agate, carved silver and carved jade were used. With the arrival of the British and a need to assert political authority and domain, Indian courts of the eighteenth century embellished hookahs even further: jade inlaid with diamonds, and enamelled using gold wire.

One of the most expensive hookahs that exist today only in India are the Malabar hookahs. Three hundred years ago, when hookahs were made for wealthy Indian and Yemeni merchants, Malabar hookahs were made simply using coconut shells as a vase. In time brass replaced coconut shells. What is unique about these hookahs is that the entire hookah including the base, the cup and the holder for the pipe, is made of carved brass, giving the hookah the appearance of one solid object. These hookahs, crafted by the Moosari coppersmith community remain one of the most coveted hookah designs in the world even today.

INLAND LETTER
The first air letter in the world

Date of Origin: 1848
Material: Paper, Ink

In 1911, French pilot Henri Piquet flew with 6,500 letters in a biplane from Allahabad for a distance of six miles to Naini, making this the first official airmail in the world. The letters he was carrying though were first issued on 15 September 1848 at post offices in Bombay, Calcutta, Delhi and Madras and were called the inland letters. They cost 2 annas and came with a self-printed stamp. Their low cost did not allow for registration and their weight at 3 grams meant that they could not hold anything inside except what was written on them. Sometimes drawbacks can lead to innovation – their weight and economy made them perfect for airlifting.

Despite the fact that India had the most extensive postal system in the world, the inland letter was slow and the inland air letter was too expensive. So there was a third option, the inland postcard. But the inland letter is what actually served as the provenance for the two others. It was also the classiest way to write. Its design was a simple postcard that when folded and flaps sealed, made the communication private in the most efficient way. Palm-sized, it had three finger-sized flaps, one each on the left and right and one on the top. Its official name was the inland letter card. The inland letter was sky blue, the inland air letter white with a red and blue striped border and the inland postcard camel in colour. Of all three, the blue inland letter was used the most.

Today, the inland letter keeps the country of over a billion in touch through 160,000 post offices delivering a 158 billion mails every year linking the country through 600,000 letter boxes. These reach the thickest of forests and the farthest of villages. (The highest village in the mountains at 4700 metres with the postal code 172114 is in Sikkim.)

When the postal system was put into place, it was not without its perils as postmen had to watch out for wild animals and bandits in the areas they traversed. In the 1920s, sometimes a drummer went alongside him escorted by two torchbearers and two archers after nightfall.

The blue inland letters was how one communicated with the cousins. There was usually a lot to share, which meant scribbling on the side-flaps in the tiniest handwriting possible. Boarding schools provided inland letters to communicate with families and friends. An inland letter from Dehradun to New Delhi would take anywhere between 1–4 days, and to Madras, now Chennai, or Bangalore, now Bengaluru, would take about 4–6 days. If the ink-pen leaked while writing, it meant starting all over again.

Even though contemporary India prefers the use of e-mail and instant messages for private correspondence, inland letters still exist and have taken on a new role. Swanky advertising for just about any product can now be printed on an inland letter, keeping the postal service busy. The classic version is still on sale at all post offices around the country for Rs 2.50.

JAIPUR FOOT

A rapid fit limb that permits normal sitting, squatting and climbing

Date of Origin: 1969
Material: Plastic, rubber

In 1968, a Jaipur-based NGO created an artificial limb that became commonly known as the Jaipur Foot. It is different from Western prosthetics as it offers a solution for basic foot movement – not only walking with shoes and sitting on chairs, but also walking barefoot on uneven terrain, and squatting or sitting crossed-legged, necessary to the lifestyle in India. Besides, this prosthetic takes an hour to build, a few hours to fit and lasts for more than four years. Easily obtained raw materials like rubber, wood and plastic pipes ensured that it cost an average of fifty dollars, making it affordable compared to other expensive prosthetics. Thus, with its extreme mobility and affordability, it changed the lives of millions of amputees in India and around the world. The limb is a classic case of frugal design, where scarcity of resources fuels creativity.

The creation of Jaipur foot was serendipitous – the result of a collaboration between craftsman Ram Chander and orthopaedist Pramod Karan Sethi. Chander got the idea at a bicycle repair shop in Jaipur in 1969 as he watched the tyres being retreaded with vulcanized rubber. He took the idea of hinging vulcanized rubber to a wooden limb to Sethi who gave it the mechanics, bringing about the movement of a human leg. This resulted in the creation of a prosthetic limb, and the foundation of an organization called the Bhagwan Mahaveer Viklang Sahayata Samiti (BMVSS) by a social activist D.R. Mehta. Since then they have served the world's poorest and largest population in need of limbs.

The Jaipur Foot technology has three vital components: a prosthetic foot, a knee joint, and a socket and shank. The forefoot and the heel are made of sponge rubber, and the ankle is made of a block of wood. All these are cast in a rubber that gives this prosthetic the appearance of a natural foot, thus giving confidence to the wearer.

In 2009, a research collaboration with Stanford University resulted in the Stanford–Jaipur Knee. It is made of light, strong and self-lubricated nylon, making it easy for the wearer to squat or kneel due to its flexibility and stable knee-like articulation.

The limb is very easy to fit. Its sockets and shank use a light weight and seamless material called High Density Polyethylene Pipe (HDPE). HDPE's natural skin tone does not need any cosmetic cover and its shape as a pipe is closer to the shape of a leg than the sheet used in other prosthetics. To make the limb, the HDPE is simply draped over the patient's remaining limb to get the exact replica of the socket. While most centres around the world use lamination or thermoformed sheets, the socket and shank using these HDPE pipes happens in a single step, thus reducing price, production and waiting time.

The BMVSS fits 16,000 limbs every year in twenty-seven countries. The patients usually arrive from far at one of the many centres and spend the night with other patients sharing meals and experiences. The prosthetic is then designed and fitted over a few hours the next day. As D.R. Mehta puts it, 'the amputees crawl in its centres with sorrow and walk out with all smiles'.

JAIPURI RAZAI

The cotton quilt famous for its beautiful patterns

Date of Origin: Around 1700 CE
Material: Cotton wool, cotton

In any ordinary quilt, the cotton clumps over time, thus thinning the razai and driving the air out. This is when quilts are usually discarded; but not Jaipuri razais. Every year, prior to the onset of winter, the cotton wool in any other razai is removed and carded again in a process similar to how it is initially carded, by careful combing. However, not in the case of Jaipuri razai. This razai is a great example of sustainable living. It can be used for a very long time, one of the many reasons why it is the first choice that comes to mind when buying a quilt.

The first Jaipuri razai was made for the Maharaja of Jaipur around 250 years ago. It was different from other quilts. Instead of the ordinary clumpy cotton, it had feather-light cotton that took months to cure. This fine filling is what gave warmth to the razai, making it like a 'pashmina' of quilts. But it was not just warm, a hand-block printed cover with detailed floral and foliate motifs was slipped on the delicate cotton. The cover made the bedding an object to be enjoyed even when not in use. When created they were used only in the palaces of Rajasthani royalty. But gradually they were smuggled out of palaces and into the homes of wealthy merchants. This is how they became popular. Today the Jaipuri razai dresses up beds around the world because it is light enough to use in the summer and warm enough to use in the winter.

The quilt's noted warmth comes from its painstakingly carded cotton stuffing. Carding is a special occupation, practised by communities of carders. These master craftsmen buy the freshest cotton crop and then card away all the debris from the cotton. At the Razai bazaar in Jaipur where generations of families have been carders, a kilo of cotton weighs not more than 100 grams after a whole week of carding. Most Jaipuri quilts are thus feather light; a double quilt weighs under a kilo.

Once the cotton is ready, a shell is prepared. A single quilt needs six metres and a double one around eleven metres of cloth for the shell. The surface of this cotton is printed with animals, flowers, leaves, stripes and other geometric motifs using wooden printing blocks. Each quilt takes around three months to make. While the basic design with the carding technique remains unchanged, the cover reflects evolving trends. For example, the foliate motifs have given way to quilted velvet covers that are considered both beautiful and contemporary. Jaipuri quilts have found homes around the world. It is this continuous evolution of patterns that has ensured that the demand for these quilts grows every year.

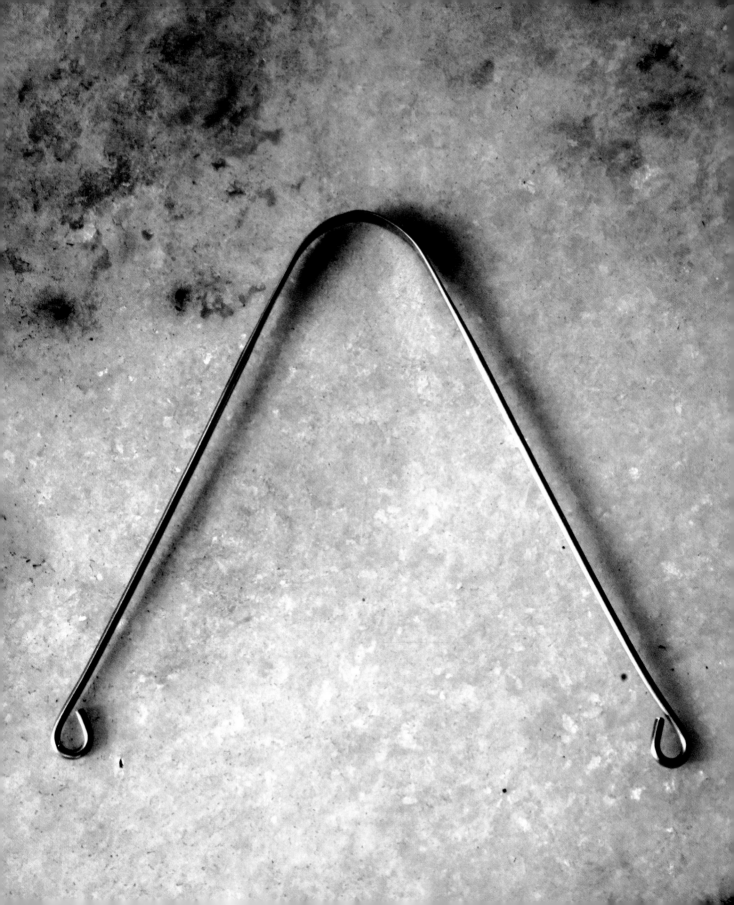

JEEBHEE

Tongs to keep the tongue clean

Date of Origin: Unknown
Material: Metal, plastic

Dental hygiene is not just a result of using a toothbrush and toothpaste but also scraping the tongue. In India, the idea of both the teeth and the tongue being part of dental hygiene has been around for a long time.

Tongue cleaning was part of the cleansing ritual of yoga. Yoga was not esoteric and involved normal and everyday ablutions for a better life. Obstructed cavities meant being unable to perceive the world clearly, so a daily cleansing ritual of the nose, ears and mouth was prescribed. Of this, dental hygiene involved brushing the teeth followed by tongue scraping and mouth washing. Oil pulling techniques, an important part of Ayurvedic cleansing involved the swishing of oil in the mouth in order to 'pull' out toxins from the stomach. Cleaning the tongue thoroughly of the swished oil was part of this therapy.

In Ayurveda, of which yoga is a part, excessive deposit of tartar and bacteria on the teeth and tongue is considered a sign of dietary imbalance. The tongue is therefore reflective of the general health of a person.

For an Ayurvedic doctor, the condition of the tongue is one of the sixteen symptoms he checks to diagnose an imbalance. To remove this tartar and bacteria, a U-shaped metal strip is passed on the tongue's surface from the back to the front. In time, metal was replaced with plastic because it would get corroded with use. While there is much advertising for toothbrushes and toothpastes, there is none for these brightly patterned long flat plastic tongue cleaners. Tartar removal through tongue cleaning is the reason why few Indians never need to get their teeth whitened.

The tongue cleaner is both original and brilliant as it makes the tongue look good. Even though characteristic of Indian oral hygiene, it has travelled around the world. Though it is doubtful that it is used in the West, it is believed that the Romans who had an extensive culture of ablutions scraped their tongues, whereas the wealthy Europeans in the eighteenth and nineteenth centuries too practised it frequently. The Japanese continue to be fervent tongue cleaners.

JHANJH

Brass cymbals bringing light into music

Date of Origin: 700 CE
Material: Metal, cotton thread

Jhanjhs are small cymbals that are keepers of time in Indian classical music. They are like a stopwatch that measures *tal*, literally a clap. *Tal*, made of two words, is used to create rhythmic compositions and is a unique feature of Indian music. It comes from the tandava dance of Shiva that expresses the cycle of birth, preservation and destruction. Lasya that is Parvati's dance is more graceful and gentle than Shiva's and creates *laya* or tempo that is the gap between one beat and the next. *Tal* means to fix, find or establish a time order or cycle on which a song, an instrumental piece or dance is based. To measure it is the primary function of the jhanjh.

Small enough to fit into the palm of the hand, this percussion instrument is the basis of Indian classical music. It consists of two small discs joined together by a string which is wrapped around the finger while playing. Jhanjhs are made either by shaping brass or by sand-casting. They are struck frontally or on the sides, and playing them mimics clapping. This is often in variations of beats of three – clap, then clap again and slide – this creates a fixed time lag. While the clapping can sound relentlessly energetic, the vibration created by the slide is a contrast; it is severe, beautiful and almost trance-like. This giddiness that is not romantic is rare in musical instruments. This is the reason why jhanjhs are used in devotional songs; they express fervour.

The clapping of jhanjhs is also a part of military bands in India, just as larger cymbals are in the West. These bands also called Naubats were considered the most powerful form of Indian music. Consisting only of percussion and wind instruments, Naubat was played five times a day at the time of prayers and also sunrise and sunset.[10] It was part of bands seated on elephants and would herald the arrival of the king or his victory. Platforms for the Naubat are still found at the entrance of all palaces around the country including the Rashtrapati Bhavan in New Delhi.

The sound made by the jhanjh has a flexible pulse. The beat of three has many possibilities due to innumerable variations, vibrations and dynamic dips. It results in a crescendo when the clapping gives way only to a rhythmic chiming along its rims. This crescendo is what Matang Muni, a seventh-century music critic, described as a sound that glows on its own.[11] Sound that is luminous is music. Jhanjhs are the smallest of musical instruments but they lend luminosity and a deliberate tempo to any musical piece. The silence produced when their sound stops is also considered a sound. Ancient Indians referred to it as the Naad Brahma, or the unstruck sound from which all sounds are born.

JHOLA
A cloth bag that fits everything

Date of Origin: Unknown
Material: Cloth, thread

The jhola is a smart collapsible bag made of cloth. Light weight, and designed to carry everything from books and pens to fruits and vegetables, its versatility has made it a favourite not only in India but also worldwide where it serves as the humble forefather of the now ubiquitous and fashionable tote bag. The etymology of the word jhola connotes an action of 'swinging' like a cradle. In some languages it refers to a fakir's bag, a nest of eggs or a feeding bag for cattle and a man's testicles.

The single strap jhola was an activist's accessory made famous by participants in the freedom struggle. Mahatma Gandhi carried all his belongings in two of them that he slung across in a neat cross from both shoulders on his bare chest during the twenty-three day and three hundred kilometre Salt March from Ahmedabad to Dandi. Since then journalists, social activists, scholars, and pundits have carried jhola bags. Jholas, thus, carried with them a message of resistance.

Jholas inspired hobos and totes that are today the world's most popular bag forms. But while the jhola hangs from the shoulder with a single strap, the hobo has two. This is because the hobo comes from the two-strap jhola. This jhola was less high-minded than the khadi one that Gandhi carried; it was a practical beast of burden. Made of tough canvas and burlap, it transported incense, soaps, tea and rice from wholesalers to stores.

They had on them advertising for these products borrowed from mythology like Krishna eating biscuits, or movies like Mother India with a sack of rice. This rich canvas of images caught the attention of hippies. In the 1960s as hippies came to India to escape from the Vietnam War, they took back with them the kohlapuri chappal and the jhola. Jholas were a canvas of jute and burlap, which the hippies had embroidered with elephants, camels, peacocks, flowers, birds, trees, leaves, temples, and monuments.

But so far the jhola has not left the realm of hippie fashion. In the 1980s, Levi's jeans became cult clothing. They were worn with a tie-dyed T-shirt with a jhola that completed the eclectic style. It was because the jhola was part of this mixed styling and added colour to denim that it became an international fashion item. The Japanese high street picked it up in the early 1990s as it matched the vibrant mood of the trance-loving Tokyoites.

In its international version, it was made in soft suede. Decorative elements, such as embroidery and fringes stayed on. That is how the humble jhola went on to become a fashion favourite. French designer Vanessa Bruno made hers embroidered with sequins into a very popular accessory that sold millions. Jholas and hobos are effortless and personal. All those who have an 'It-bag' also own its anti-thesis: the hobo.

JUTTI / MOJRI

Protective ballerina slip-ons for both men and women

Date of Origin: Unknown
Material: Leather, sequins, cotton, wool, silk thread

Before the jutti became fashionable, it was a simple footwear made for farmers and herders to work in the fields or graze herds in the arid desert landscape. Juttis originated in the two states of Haryana and Rajasthan and this is where most of them are still made. To the fun loving world population they are like ballerinas meant for feminine style and comfort, but for the farmers of this vast, tough geography that is sandy, rocky and thorny, these shoes are designed to be thick, sturdy and protective. Its evolution is a simple innovative response to the harsh environment around; it is organic and stylish too.

Their making is simple: leather uppers are traced out on camel skin, cut out and embroidered. Goat or buffalo skin is also used sometimes. After being richly embroidered, they are stitched on to the sole that has been cut out of buffalo hide. The soles are made in a manner similar to the kohlapuri chappal; a few layers are glued together. Much before Christian Louboutin adopted the red soles for his coveted shoes, juttis already had them. Both the soles and the insole are painted a bright pink or red to match the embroidery on the upper; backs and heels are optional.

Their design is unique in that they contradict the classic shoe design. Firstly, they are made unidirectional.

The reasons are unknown but slipping on the right or the left foot was simply not much of a concern. Instead the tough terrain around inspired their design. The thick embroidery or wool pompons (that tower a few centimetres in height in the tauranwari juttis from Sindh) on the uppers were not just for style, it protected the feet from thorny shrubbery in the hills. The slim, tongue-shaped sole of the shoe, that barely covers the foot entirely, was left open to easily throw out sand that got caught while walking. As the sole is visible while walking, it also was richly decorated, a sophistication that is not afforded to the most expensive of shoes even today.

The toes could be rounded or pointed for daily use, and curled toes that end in a sharp point on the foot are reserved for special occasions. With the revival of interest in indigenous fashion, juttis travelled to the city in the 1980s where they were just the perfect footwear to go with salwar kurtas for both men and women. As the leather wears, juttis become soft. They are constructed to sit low on the ankle like a mule and leave the toes half bare, giving the feeling of a fine sock, barely there. This aesthetic attracted international designers like Tory Burch who always has a jutti inspiration in every collection.

KAJAL

Home-made kohl to enhance the beauty of the eyes

Date of Origin: Unknown
Material: Kohl

Kajal is the cosmetic that India has given to the world, proof of which lies in the fact that every big international cosmetics company has created a kajal stick of its own. The cosmetic that accentuates the eye on its hood is called the eye-liner, and that which traces the bottom is kajal, also referred to as kohl in the Middle East. Professional stylists use the eye-liner to define the lids and kajal to give the eye depth. But in India, its birthplace, it's not just an adornment, it's also a ritual born out of a therapeutic practice.

The 1500 BC Ayurveda guide *Sushruta Samhita* elaborates the making of kajal. The purest kajal is made at home. A small lamp is lit with castor oil and a cotton wick. The soot is collected on a silver spatula and mixed in a drop of castor oil or pure ghee and applied to the eyes. Lamps in silver are preferred due to their anti-bacterial quality, and the shallow bowl where the soot is deposited has a lid that pivots open or shuts keeping it free from impurities. The object for making kajal is in itself a work of art, as it is made just for collecting soot for the eyes. But kajal is also medicinal and various recipes used to make it reflect this, such as an extract from the stem and root of the barberry plant, turmeric powder, almonds, and neem leaves. The wick is dipped in a solution made of these ingredients. Tears help rejuvenate the eyes and kajal is made to speed up this process and keep them healthy and disease free. This medicinal application turned into a beauty ritual.

The centuries-old gesture of a mother applying kajal to her baby's eyes or a young girl defining her eyes with kajal taken from the spatula with the tip of the ring finger remains firmly entrenched in India. Both baby girls and boys wear kajal. They are called teet and made of boiled parijaat flowers. But the formula for children is different as it contains no camphor. Traditionally men too applied kohl. The most famous character known for smouldering kohl-lined eyes is actor Jagdeep from Ramesh Sippy's cult 1975 film, *Sholay*. Called Surma Bhopali, he was famous for his trademark hat and smouldering kohl-rimmed gaze. The name stuck throughout his illustrious career. Surma, the paste he applied is another formulation like kajal that uses collyrium powdered on a stone with herbs.

To an Indian, the act of a woman applying this thick dark paste to her eyes from a kajal lamp will always be considered an act of romance. The tenth-century sculptured temples of Khajuraho celebrate this with a series of sculptures. In the Braj region where the cowherd-god Krishna reigned, there is a place called Anjanokh where Krishna is believed to have adorned his lover Radha's eyes with kajal. The story is enacted every year at the region's annual centuries-old forest festival. In all the six classical Indian dance forms, eye movements form an important part of its extensive repertoire. Kajal is the unbroken thread between the India of treatises and today.

KALNIRNAY
The world's most secular calendar

Date of Origin: 1993
Material: Paper

Calendars are the design of life, and few objects are at the core of everyday life as much as them. To design a calendar one needs mathematics and astronomy, but to make it useful one needs a civilization whose daily preoccupations are in response to the movements of the sun, the moon, the planets, day, night, and the changing seasons. The standardized Indian national calendar used today is a combination of a lunar calendar and a Gregorian solar calendar. While this might be the official calendar, the most widely used almanac in India is a lunar calendar called the Kalnirnay (founded in 1973 by an astrologer Jayantrao Salgaonkar), with twenty million copies distributed in seven languages. It is referred to as the modern 'Hindu' calendar, but in reality it also prints important dates from the Muslim, Judaic, Christian, and Parsee traditions.

The Kalnirnay takes the Hindu calendar as its base (it is named Hindu calendar only because most people who use it are Hindus). The Hindu calendar in effect is a collective name for two of the most widely used calendars in India – the Vikram Samvat (started during the reign of King Vikramaditya, with the year zero at 57 BCE) and the Saka calendar (the official civil calendar that starts at year zero 78 CE). According to Saka, a year consists of twelve months and starts in spring with the month Chaitra (March–April) and finishes in Phalgun (February–March).

It was the deeply secular Emperor Akbar who laid down the traditions of a hybrid calendar by proposing the Tarikh-ilahi, a joint calendrical system reflecting the major religions. The system did not stay longer than him but his secular idea since then has benefitted modern calendars like the Kalnirnay.

Kalnirnay calendars are similar to the Gregorian calendars in that every season has ninety days and the year has four seasons. Each month consists of twenty-nine to thirty days depending upon the movement of the moon. So, religious festivals like Diwali and Holi are mainly based on the lunar Kalnirnay. The general system consists of twelve months and thirty days with a thirteenth month added every five years. It is unclear how this similarity with the Gregorian calendar arose, but the ancient Greeks (whose knowledge forms the basis of this calendar) and the ancient Indian mathematicians have a well-documented exchange knowledge of calculations and accounts.

But no calendar is based on religion alone. India's communal diversity has played a role in the existence of the various calendars, however, its long mathematical tradition of numbering and calculating combined with its historical precision in astronomy has also led to the calculation of months and years in the calendars. Whatever the method that was adopted, keeping current has always been a hallmark of Indian calendars. Today, it is not just the Kalnirnay paper version but also the pocket diaries, mobile and tablet applications that keep track of over three hundred national celebrations and festivals of all religions – making it the most secular calendar.

KARAHI

A metal wok that is a must in every Indian kitchen

Date of Origin: Unknown
Material: Metal, aluminium, Teflon

The word 'karahi' refers to the bowl shape of a wok-like utensil. It is different from other woks of Asia as it has two handles in the form of round iron rings riveted directly to a scooped, unpainted iron bowl. This simple addition of handles is crucial for the two stages of heat necessary in Indian cooking, high temperature for deep frying the spices and moderate temperature for vegetables or grains that are then added on to these spices. A karahi is a clever cooking utensil by being two dishes in one, thus preserving the even taste of Indian cooking.

Karahi's basic function is deep frying dry spices, the first step of cooking using its deep shape. The handles along with the weight of the bowl keep it sturdy during this heat-intensive phase. In an iron karahi the heat is unevenly distributed necessitating constant stirring. This is all the more desirable as only in a karahi can the flavour of fully fried spices perfume the grain or vegetable that is added later. Cooking in a karahi compared to a flat-bottomed pan evens the flavour of something as simple as fried rice. In a frying pan the taste stays in pockets, and in a karahi it is smooth because the rice can be turned more easily. This even

flavour is a signature of Indian cuisine. The Lonely Planet describes the karahi as a macho cast-iron version of the Chinese wok. But karahi recipes are flavourful and delicate – karahi shrimp, karahi chicken and karahi lamb. If boned or diced meat is tossed in a karahi with fresh ground spices and chopped herbs, it makes the meat really tender.

Archaeologists and historians have been unable to find out exactly when the karahi first began to be used, but it is well known that Indians have been adept at ironmongery since well before eighth century BCE. Many historians consider India the first iron civilization. Most karahis are still made of iron, which gave way to stainless steel and aluminium in the 1950s and then to a non-stick smoother surface of Teflon in the 1990s.

As karahis are handmade, they can be customized to any desired size. Large ones have a diameter of close to a metre and the smallest ones with a diameter of fifteen centimetres are used for cooking halwa. But in most kitchens it's the decades-old iron ones that are still preferred, it's constant use is believed to add taste to the home chef's cooking.

KOHLAPURI CHAPPAL

Recyclyed footwear that became fashionable

Date of Origin: mid-1970s, Kolhapur, Maharashtra
Material: Leather, thread

Kohlapuri chappals are the world's cheapest and most popular recycled footwear. The quaint towns of Kohlapur and neighbouring Miraj, in western India, are the country's oldest centres for leather tanning and footwear. Twenty-five thousand leather shoemakers belonging to the Chamaar caste of tanners and leather work here.

The first Kohlapuri chappal was made by the Chamaar community in the mid-1970s, for themselves and other poor tanners of the area, from scraps of discarded leather salvaged from the factories. These beige-coloured, flat slippers, that hold the foot in place with one thick decorated instep connected to the loop of the big toe with a thong, use the discarded leather pieced together with clay made from a fine-grained black soil taken from the regions' rice fields. Embellishments in most Kolhapuri chappals are kept minimal except for a flamboyant, short crimson silk floss tassel in the centre of the instep; sometimes there is also a bit of embroidery with zari or gold thread, which adds excitement to an otherwise understated design.

The chappal's superbly ingenious design and its affordable price appealed to the masses. A must-have with nomadic hippies of the era, it became equally popular amongst the urban elite. In the late 1970s the chappal cost under a dollar each and became an iconic fashion item worldwide. In America they became popular as the 'buffalo sandal'; in Europe every fashionable Parisienne owned at least a pair. And Indians introduced and bought Kohlapuris in every conceivable colour – from solid black, reds, greens, yellows and blues, to the more recent ones in neon colours.

In the boom years of the 1990s, fashion's demand for the latest colours and diverse styles led to the creation of the 'designer Kohlapuri'. Malini Ramani, a favourite Indian fashion designer, painted them silver and added a towering wedge to make her creation a night club staple. In contrast to their mono-chromatic humble origins, the prize pieces of Kohlapuri chappals can be rainbow coloured. A parrot green cross-strap slipper for men, with in-step shading from moss green to leafy green, a wild mustard yellow with a woven big toe, shows how these chappals have borrowed from fashion. And responding to the trend for Japanese style tabi shoes, there are chappals with a separate cut out for each of the five fingers of the toe. The original humbler version continues to be a national favourite and a treasured keepsake for any foreigner visiting Colaba Causeway in Bombay. Contrary to what footwear-sellers say, they are neither elegant, nor very comfortable, until broken in – yet, the world has a permanent love affair with the Kohlapuris.

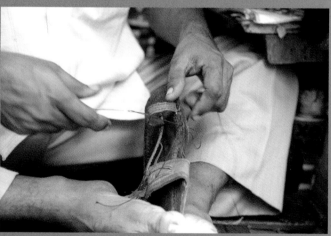

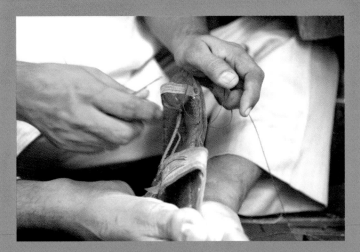
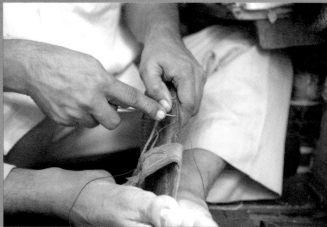

KULHAD
Simple and sustainable earthen cup

Date of Origin: 2600 BCE, Indus valley
Material: Earthen clay

Kulhads are not just a plain form of hand-moulded earth, they also embody sophisticated sustainable design enmeshed with a tradition that is as old as the Indus Valley Civilization.

Kulhad cups are the simplest form of pottery that can be 'thrown' on a potter's wheel. The only raw material required is the sediment deposited at the bottom of the river bed. Removing the sediment prevents the river from flooding. Clay is prepared from this sediment by extracting excess water and course debris. The potter places a lump of this clay on the wheel and deftly moulds it by applying pressure with his fingers. The cup shape is then neatly sliced off the wheel and laid out to dry in the sun. This dry, ash-coloured, raw form with a smooth wall is placed in the community kiln that is fuelled by straw or cow dung sourced from nearby farmers. Once firmly baked, washing off the ash and grime of the kiln reveals the rich orange hue of a good kulhad. The water also tightens the clay making it sufficiently waterproof. But as kulhads are unglazed, any liquid poured into them will eventually be absorbed by the clay making them humid after use. Hindus therefore consider clay vessels unhygienic for a second use.

For the potters who make kulhads, chaiwalas on the dense Indian railways network are their biggest clients, as the latter have been serving passengers onboard since the first train services started in India in the mid-nineteenth century. But despite the million kulhads of tea sold every day, these kulhads remain unofficial, because officially the Indian Railways buys all its catering necessities from industrial vendors in units of millions. As kulhads are handmade, most potters mould only about seventy a day. These are sold directly to the chaiwalas on country station platforms. Inside the train, paradoxically, passengers are forced to put up with plastic cups which are totally unpopular as they don't carry the taste of authenticity. But to the railways, serving in plastic kulhads was actually not a choice. Kulhad-making is not practised all over the country, for example in the South there were no sources to respond to the railways enquiries. Kulhads are also fragile resulting in transit and handling damage. And as they are handmade, their size and capacity cannot be standardized. This is the reason why plastic kulhads are served on board officially and kulhads by tea vendors unofficially.

Despite tea being served in plastic cups onboard, kulhads still epitomize the pleasure of a long Indian train journey: on a three-thousand-kilometre trip from Assam to Kanyakumari, five days can be spent catching up on unread paperbacks, day-dreaming, and smelling the fragrant scent of rain on dry ground – all the while eating hard boiled eggs and drinking countless cups of sweet kulhad chai. After drinking, the kulhad is thrown out of the window of the speeding train where it is smashed to smithereens on the tracks. Thus the kulhad goes back to the earth it was originally harvested from.

KUMKUM DABBI

Little boxes to store vermillion

Date of Origin: Unknown
Material: Wood, steel, ivory

In traditional India, cosmetics were kept in boxes called shringar-daans. They served as vanity cases and had compartments, each one for storing different cosmetics; some cosmetics like vermillion would be kept in this case in its own special box. The vanity case also contained other things like perfume containers and kohl dispensers but a great amount of care was showered on the design of vermillion boxes or sindoor-daans. After all, they contained sindoor that is a marker of every Hindu woman's marriage. Even today, in some weddings, the sindoor-daan is included in a bride's vanity case.

A sindoor-daan is small and fits neatly into the palm. In its design, the country's long tradition of miniature paintings has played a role. Some of the craftspeople who painted on a small scale were also adept at carving and painting small objects often in a whimsical manner borrowing from their imagination as painters. The most playful amongst these boxes were shaped in the form of vegetables and fruits like eggplants and mangoes. The rounded bodies of vegetables were the ideal form of containers to store powder in. Designs were drawn on ivory with a pencil in an exact copy of the fruit or vegetable in a miniature form. The boxes also had

curved, geometric and foliate designs. Amongst all sindoor-daans the ivory ones were most elaborate. But ivory as a material was expensive and this is where the compact shape of the sindoor-daan was helpful. In time as ivory was banned this tradition died, but its small size also allowed for experiment with other materials like silver, wood or lac.

Today, bright wooden sindoor-daans are most common and an integral part of Hindu wedding ceremonies. They are turned on a lathe on which a rapidly rotating piece of wood is shaped with a chisel to create parts of the box that are in the form of cylinders, spheres and cones.[12] Most of them are compact and hardly have a diameter of more than three centimetres. Their caps are even smaller. To shape them a bow string that is operated by hand or foot is used. After colouring red, green and black, they are polished using a combination of dried kevda leaf and oil, which adds lustre to their finish. As an object, sindoor-daans are small but they bring joy and colour to the vanity case. Nowadays kohl dispensers have given way to kajal pencils. But sindoor-daans whether made in wood, silver or simply plastic stay current.

KURTA PYJAMA

A short tunic and trousers designed to serve as both inner and outerwear

Date of Origin: 1 BCE
Material: Cotton, silk, khadi

Kurtas are worn during the day as formal wear and then at night to sleep in. In most cultures day and night time clothes are designed differently. This adaptability of the kurta is because it is the easiest of shirt forms –collarless, with long sleeves, side slits and a front opening till the chest. A kurta is always worn with loose drawstring pyjamas. It is indispensable in daily life and used by everyone, from the common man to politicians to priests.

The word 'kurta' is believed to come from the word 'kurtaka' that in Turkish and Persian languages refers to a short close-fitting tunic. There are various claims to its ancient origins, but the kurta as we know it today was born in the eighteenth century in the courts of Awadh. Awadhi aristocracy was innovative with clothes. So this was a fashionable modification to the 'nima', a close-fitting tunic for men that was worn then.

In its original version, the kurta was the same as it is today – white embroidery on a fine white cloth, but worn mostly under coats for almost a century. Awadhis in the nineteenth century made it elegant giving it various sizes, lengths and openings. It stayed fitted on the top, the cuts at the bottom created volume and slits on the side meant that it was airy and comfortable to sleep in while being elegant enough for outerwear. This is also why women adopted the kurta. It is believed that English tailors took it back with them to London, where from the 1880s onwards they started proposing it as the ideal sleepwear, thus upstaging the nightshirt.

Kurtas and pyjamas can be made of cotton, silk or the most iconic of materials: khadi. In 1915, hand-spun and hand-woven khadi clothes became part of the items that symbolized the struggle to create an autonomous India. While Mahatma Gandhi himself preferred to wear a dhoti, his compatriots like Vallabhbhai Patel, Chakravarti Rajagopalachari and Maulana Abul Kalam Azad, all donned the kurta pyjama. They were from different parts of the country but wore the same united dress.

Around half a century later fashion once again became restless and kurtas got shortened to a kurti, a style that started in Punjab where kurtas were not borrowed from the Awadhis and were being worn before their time. The kurta pyjama is also referred to as the 'Punjabi suit'. Alberuni, the scribe who came with Mahmud of Ghazni to India in 1000 CE, writes about the 'kurtaka' as worn with openings both on the right and left sides. The illustrated manuscripts *Chandanaya* painted in 1525–50 CE show the lovers Laur and Chanda with Laur dressed in what seems like Alberuni's 'kurtaka'.

In the 1980s, women gave the kurti a twist. In its newest avatar, it was shorter and tighter than ever before. The length was mid-thigh and accentuated the voluminous pyjamas that were worn with them. This length was longer than the Western shirt for women and breezier too. Thus it was adopted by international fashion as resort-wear. It could be worn poolside in the most sensual way and is a form that has been adopted by every fashion designer around the world.

LOTA

A metal pot with a simple design and multiple uses

Date of Origin: 2300 BCE, Daimabad
Material: Metals, plastic, clay

Designers Charles and Ray Eames on their visit to India in 1958 remarked: 'Of all the objects we have seen and admired during our visits to India, the lota, that simple vessel of everyday use, stands out as perhaps the greatest, the most beautiful. The village women have a process which, with the use of tamarind and ash, each day turns this brass into gold. But how would one go about designing a lota?'[13]

The use of lota (a word with no English equivalent) has been epic. A shapely spherical object, its scooped neck makes it easy to hold between fingers. Traditionally made of copper or brass, possessing an orange hue to a bright yellow or a subdued golden patina, the lota dazzles and makes all Indian kitchens glow. A multi-purpose metal vessel for all walks of Indian life, it is used for fetching water, performing religious rituals, and even practising yoga.

It functions as a tumbler, water container, canister, jug, and a stackable container, all in one. Indian consumer fetishism combined with Brahmanical Puritanism ensures that individual lotas are used for distinct purposes even if identical; this results in an attractive array of lotas in most homes: a large one for storing water; a smaller one for bathing; or, a miniature lota for the home shrine that stores sacred water from the river Ganges. The lota is an undisputed tribute to its unknown creator. As Charles and Ray Eames said, 'they are well-engineered, often containing the optimum amount of liquid to be fetched, carried, and stored.'[14] Hydraulic dynamics are exacting and nothing spills when being poured.

Both the sacred and profane worlds convey themselves through the lota. In Indian mythology, Lord Shiva's lota is distinct with its handle – it's in this lota that he keeps the entire river Kaveri. The lota used for yoga has a spout to help cleanse the body. Thus, the lota is the carrier of the exalted and the completely desacralized world, all in one.

The lota's usage is centuries old, but its relevance in daily chores today, especially in rural India, has not diminished. In cities, the lota has been transformed. In the 1990s, colourful and inexpensive plastic lotas joined the traditional ranks of copper and brass ones.

In the domicile of the urban aesthete, the lota has gained new respectability. Its perfect curves and beautiful material can substitute for lamp bases or flower vases. One could argue that the lota is now passé considering the variety of canisters, jugs, water bottles and other available containers, but that is the point – the lota is all of this combined. Surveying the country proves that lota is still and shall always be au courant.

IDLI PATHRAM

A utensil to prepare India's favourite breakfast, idlis

Date of Origin: 1950s
Material: Stainless steel, aluminium

If one were to divide India along a food fault line, it would have to be a North–South one: the North with its chai–samosa and the South with its idli–dosa. And yet, this line is by no means set in stone. It's the Tamilians who have taken the idli northwards, and beyond Indian shores to America, where it is sold as a diet meal with the perfect mix of carbohydrates and proteins. But it's the North that gave idli-making a modern twist: smartly pressure-cooking the idlis in a custom-made stainless steel stand called the idli pathram. The utensil consists of two–three trays put together with a steel rod and a screw. The holes in the trays help in steaming the idlis.

Behind the idli-maker lays the story of stainless steel. From the early 1950s, due to huge government subsidies the steel industry flourished and stainless steel started filtering into Indian kitchens, first in Delhi, Bombay and Poona, and then Madras. In the kitchen, stainless steel took over traditional brass, bronze, copper and tin vessels largely due to the former's affordability and the high maintenance of polishing and cleaning required by traditional metals.

The traditional idli pathram, made of iron, was an important part of any Tamil-Brahmin kitchen. All kitchens were equipped with many different sizes of this utensil. In the big cities like Delhi and Bombay, idlis were eaten only at south Indian specialty restaurants. The growing popularity of these restaurants that offered a cuisine different from the north Indian's daily palate of wheat, rice and vegetables meant that the idli-maker found its way into traditional north Indian kitchens and Sunday afternoon lunches. Due to easy access to stainless steel in the 1970s, steel idli pathrams started being sold in the markets. The convenience of being able to make idlis almost instantly in an idli-maker is what helped the tradition of the idli disperse itself far and wide.

From Lucknow in the North to Bangalore in the South, housewives spent many sunny winter afternoons with stainless steel vendors who, like door-to-door salesmen, went through every aspiring locality peddling stainless steel utensils that included idli pathrams. These purveyors followed a barter system like in indigenous communities, exchanging old and used clothes for utensils. Silk saris like Kanjivarams in the South and Banarsi brocade in the North were particularly prized. Polyester, another harbinger of modernity, came a close second. The vendors would burn the saris, and sell the residual metal zari embroidery for money. If they couldn't wrangle zari sarees, they collected clothes that they could resell at the Sunday neighbourhood bazaar.

It's in the use of utensils like the stainless steel idli-maker that the gradual transformation and modernization of a whole generation can be seen. In India, life is at once contemporary, where saving time is important and hence the use of the idli pathram in a pressure cooker, and also traditional, which means that hot idlis continue to be prepared fresh.

LPG

Liquid Petroleum Gas, the fuel of the nation

Date of Origin: 1984
Material: Iron, LPG

In India, 'gas connection' was a prized word. To have one would take years, and only divine intervention sped things up. But it was worth the wait. Chulhas or mud stoves were used in villages, which used wood or animal dung for fuel and one had to squat on the floor to cook, a smoky and messy ordeal. Kerosene, the fuel of choice for stoves in cities, was not without hazard either. It often leaked and meals were prepared slowly, only one dish at a time. So burners fuelled by Liquefied Petroleum Gas (LPG) cylinders became the definition of a modern household. The cylinder cooked many dishes simultaneously in a neat and smoke-free environment.

LPG is a mixture of hydrocarbon fuels, liquefied for easy handling in pressurized containers. It is also highly inflammable. The LPG cylinder is pressed in two pieces and then welded together to make a compact unit without any leaks. It is spray-painted in red to signal danger. (Cylinders in 'Oxford Blue' colour with a red band carry LPG meant for use in commercial and industrial establishments.) In India red cylinders are also the subsidized ones meant for households.

Many developing nations rely heavily on LPG for domestic fuel. India has the widest distribution network for this. After all, 160 million households use it, and more than twelve thousand LPG distributors home deliver nearly 3.5 million cylinders every day, catering to more than half of the country's population.

While the larger cylinders were used at homes, the smaller cylinders of 5 kilogrammes brought with them opportunities for street vendors.

The regular mode for transport of LPG cylinders from the gas agency to homes, especially in the cities, is a small-sized 'tempo-truck'. They are also delivered on bicycles modified simply and cleverly with a carrier rack particularly designed and welded at a local welding shop so that it can carry up to five cylinders instead of one.

But as any manually organized and subsidized system, delivery of cylinders provoked black market abuse. Now with the country's digital Unique Identification Number (UID) system in place, every delivery boy and tempo has an electronic portable device, and the customer pays the market price. This digitalization has resulted in a smoother stock and subsidy control.

In all developing countries including India, where LPG is used, it has been a representative of middle-class households. But in India it has touched the lives of even those who could not afford to have it in their homes. The chaiwalas provoked innovation in street commerce for the design of the stove that fitted on the cylinder. So the biggest design of the cylinder has not been in the object itself but in the adaptability of life around it. It has provoked India to be at its best and most resourceful.

MANDIRA

A churning device for milk products

Date of Origin: 5000 BCE
Material: Wood, metal, plastic

The butter-churner or mandira is a fairly common article in all cultures that use milk around the world. In India it carries with it a symbolism unusual of kitchen implements: Krishna, the most popular of all Indian divinities, is often painted as an infant holding a richly-decorated mandira dripping with butter. Churning with this mandira is an important part of Indian mythology as devas (gods) and asuras (demons) decide to use Mount Meru as the churner to churn the ocean that then reveals treasures like the pot of plenty.[15]

The representation of the mandira here seems exaggerated. It's almost unimaginable (at least the other butter-churners around the world have the very earthly occupation of making butter). But that's what is fascinating about mandiras.

Dairy-farming and the practice ofdrinking fresh milk started in India around 7500 years ago. Mandiras were used to make butter and buttermilk, but this was not their ultimate use. They had one primary use – to make ghee. Ghee is considered precious in the country; it is both a currency (Kautilya advises the collection of ghee as tax) and is believed to be the elixir of life.

Ghee is not just fatty acids, as widely believed today. It has nine important antioxidants that help keep the skin healthier. Ghee is absorbed easily by the cell membrane bringing all its intrinsic benefits and also

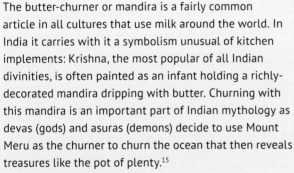

nutrients from the food cooked in it.

Mandiras are an important part of this process of making ghee. Cream collected from boiled milk is churned to make butter. Since it is difficult to store butter for long, it is often used to prepare ghee, which lasts for months. Once the excess water has been drained from the butter, it is heated on a low flame to evaporate all residual water and what is obtained is ghee. It is more stable due to the absence of milk solids and water and thus stays fresh for long. Mandiras facilitate the separation of butter from buttermilk which is then used to make ghee.

Its design is explained in mythology. The devas and the asuras have their differences, so each churns in a different direction alternatively – which is how the mandira works.The mandira is basically a stick that is held between the palms and is rotated alternatively in a clockwise and an anti-clockwise direction, the wooden blades arranged in a disk at the bottom of the stick churn and skim. The wooden axis of the mandira is that of space. The milky whiteness feels like an ocean of possibilities but needs to be churned. And the result when done long enough is butter, which finally becomes ghee. Ghee represents power, pleasure and prosperity, and all the things that everyone wants and the mandira is the all important tool.

MANGALSUTRA

A black bead necklace worn by women as a symbol of marriage

Date of Origin: Unknown
Material: Black beads in adobe, gold, diamond

The mangalsutra as it's called in north India and thaali in south India, is one of the five symbols of a married woman. A firm red bindi on the forehead, bright crimson vermillion running through in the parting of the hair, multiple red bangles on the wrists and a few toe rings – these are the other everyday adornments and empowerment of a Hindu bride. In Sanskrit the mangalsutra means an auspicious thread; this is reflected in its design of a chain with an amulet. But as is often the case in India, symbols become design forms and these forms are then individualized. The thread can be very simple like black, yellow or gold or it can be a chain with black beads or even a gold chain. But in all these designs, it's the black beads that have a recurring presence. They are made of earth because earth is believed to absorb negative energy while the amulet acts as a talisman against the 'evil eye' to safeguard the life of the husband and the couple.

Depending on the region and community, people adopt one or many versions of the mangalsutra, like the shiva lingam worn by the Iyer community, the namam and sudarshana chakra worn by the Iyengars, simpler ivory by the Punjabis and the kashitali worn by the Kannads, which consists of a gold chain strung with coral and black beads around a gold pendant. Trying to understand the design of the mangalsutra is a task, its design goes far beyond the confines of the boundaries

of states, into communities, castes and tribes, each one with a unique design. The mangalsutra as a symbol of the married woman goes far beyond the Hindus. Christian women in the southern state of Kerala, for example, have adopted the mangalsutra too. In fact every single jeweller around the country would have his own catalogue of various mangalsutra designs to chose from.

It is unknown when the mangalsutra originated. Texts from the fifteenth and sixteenth centuries have recorded the tying of the mangalsutra as part of a ritual. But the wearing of the ornament has evolved ever since into becoming, what for some is, a daily practice. Mangalsutras have been made modern with a diamond pendant or a short version that fits close to the neck. Today, the number of modern Indian women wearing the mangalsutra might have reduced considerably, but every married woman still owns one.

Can the managalsutra, a ritual object of a centuries-old society that celebrates the power of the feminine be switched to a man? Bollywood tried doing so. In the film *Ki & Ka*, the title loosely translated as 'his and hers', the female protagonist who is the bread winner of the family lovingly adorns her stay-at-home husband with a mangalsutra. But that sort of a role reversal is quite besides the point. Because the mangalsutra is a powerful expression of a certain kind of feminism that shall never go out of date.

MANGTIKA

A piece of jewellery worn on the forehead

Date of Origin: Unknown
Material: Gold, uncut diamonds, precious and semi-precious stones, peacock feathers, flowers, leaves

Though it is meant to represent the tika, the mangtika is elaborate, always curved and often with a star in the centre. In its purest version the mangtika, when worn only on the forehead, is called the *chak*. Whereas all tikas look essentially the same, the chak has numerous designs differentiated by the presence or absence of stones, beads and chains accompanied by a different name for each design, like the chak-phul being a cluster of chaks.[16] In Rajasthan the mangtika has strips that frame the edge of the hair and the forehead and often end in umbrella drop earrings. The mangtika is so important as an object that a version of it that used rubies, emeralds and pearls was presented to Edward, Prince of Wales, in 1877 by the Maharaja of Jaipur.[17]

The mangtika is actually one part of an elaborate piece of interlinked jewellery that frames the forehead and is hooked into the hair just above the ears. This is called the *shringarpatti*. When seeing a *shringarpatti* one is conditioned to recall a classical dancer in a temple with an expressive face full of precise movements. This vision is similar to that of a bride at a wedding, after all a Bharatanatyam dancer too was a bride, married to the gods.

Women throughout the country use it as an ornament for the head. But it's in the northernmost tip of the country that this design is at its extreme and is extended over the braid to cover the back of the head all the way over to the waist. It has an intensity that is almost sculptural as it is embroidered with large turquoise stones and weighty pieces of coral. In Rajasthan, like in Ladakh where this ornament is given more value than in the rest of the country, peacock feathers or even leaves are used to decorate the forehead. In the south of India, two moons accompany the mangtika and frame the head just like a hair band and are also referred to as the sun ornament for the one on the right side and the moon ornament for the one on the left.[18]

The studded, weighty objects – giving every woman a wonder woman effect – are noteworthy for the messages they send. Of course that of femininity is self evident on that list, but so is wealth and social hierarchy that have been woven in, along with braids, stones, feather, and flowers.

MASALA DABBA

A box with different compartments for storing masalas or spices

Date of Origin: Unknown
Material: Wood, stainless steel, platic, metals

India is known for its cooking with spices, after all, it produces 70 per cent of what the world consumes. The International Organization for Standardization (ISO) lists one hundred and nine spices, out of which Indian homes cook with around seven to eight at every meal. Most home chefs add spices on instinct without measuring and without any written recipe. Their stocking, however, is very organized as all the basic spices are stored in a spice box or masala dani designed so that no spice gets left out while cooking. This convenient method to store them is shared by restaurant chefs too. Most professional Indian kitchens use over fifty spices daily; the stocks are well documented in daily sheets by chefs. The spices might vary according to regions, but the method to stock them remains unchanged.

Spices are dry, and keeping them in their dried powder form in a south Indian humid environment was a challenge that only a wooden spice container could solve. Traditionally these boxes were carved slicing off a piece of the trunk of a single tree with multiple recesses, the size of a water glass, to hold different spices. Moisture filters through the wood naturally while allowing the contents to breathe. In the 1950s and 1960s all utensils in the kitchen came to be made of stainless steel, the most fashionable material in the kitchen because it always looked new. Spice boxes too changed from wood to this new material as it was also lighter and took less place in the kitchen cabinet, but its form did not change.

Every kitchen shelf is equipped with this new masala dani, a simple large round box with usually seven smaller containers. The actual contents of the box vary from home to home. After use, as none of these small containers have a lid, the whole box is covered with a round flat lid and put away till the next meal. But no spice box is complete without the mix that is today famous globally as Garam Masala; this is a mix of cloves and five or more dried spices, including cardamom, cinnamon and black pepper but never chilli – the quantity of each ingredient in the mixture varies regionally. The masala became popular as it was used to give taste (but not sting) to 'curries' for the British and then for the Japanese armies fighting in the World War I.

MURHA
A comfortable bamboo seat

Date of Origin: 2 CE
Material: Bamboo, nylon fibre

Murhas or bamboo stools have been used in India for over 2000 years without a single modification. They come in several different forms but even the simplest morha is striking not just for its hour-glass shape, but its resilient structure made only of fine strips of bamboo. At the Crystal Palace exhibition held in London in 1851, murhas were exhibited as 'examples of typical Indian household furniture'.

Murhas are made by bamboo craftsmen. Thin bamboo stalks are used to form a drum shape. This shape is twisted in the middle and the bamboo is bound with cane splits to hold the structure in place. Bamboo rings are then placed on the top and the bottom and a woven split cane seat is worked into the top ring. This slanted placement of bamboo is what makes the murha unique, providing structure and strength. The load on the seat is transferred to the rim avoiding strain on it and then shifted from the rim to the large number of thin twisted bamboo stalks that support each other and stabilize the structure.

Examples of the murha shape can be seen in Buddhist narrative art from the second century onwards. The stool or raised seating was a sign of elevated status such as that of a prince or a king. Murhas were in all likelihood used by common people too, given the widespread availability and affordability of the raw material. By the mid-nineteenth century, they became part of the standard government furniture allowance for British administrators in India and were used not so much for sitting on as for resting tired feet.[19]

More recently murhas that were only stools have been transformed into chairs by fitting them with a curved circular backrest made of the sarkanda plant. While these are widely available from itinerant vendors, their origins lie in similar bamboo chairs that were imported from China in the late eighteenth and early nineteenth centuries.[20] These are woven in a similar fashion to the murha but with crisscrossed and bound stalks. The backrests are tall, giving the whole structure a height of more than a metre, and comfortable, as they envelop the back and the sides seating up to two people. Ready availability of nylon fibre in infinite colours has given the murha variety.

Nowadays, there is often a prayer room or corner in every home with a classic murha placed in front of the shrine on which one can meditate or pray. While the basic form and method of construction has remained unchanged, the murha continues to be a part of everyday life.

MYSORE SANDAL SOAP

The world's only pure sandalwood soap

Date of Origin: 1916, Mysore
Material: Natural and identical sandalwood, lactones, soap base

Amongst the 450 tonnes of soap manufactured every year in India, the most distinguished is the Mysore sandal soap. The soap has a unique warm, milky aroma. It is made from oil extracted from sandalwood trees and is the world's only sandalwood soap.

Sandalwood is the definitive scent of India. Mysore, a small, princely city in Karnataka, 140 kilometre from Bangalore, is one of the most important producers of sandalwood oil in the world. In ancient Egypt, sandalwood imported from here was considered indispensable for perfumes. In the 1950s more than 50 per cent of international perfumes contained sandalwood notes. Today sandalwood is grown in many parts of India and in other tropical regions, including Northern Australia, however, perfumers worldwide still rate Mysore sandalwood as the finest.

In Mysore the sandalwood tree was declared a royal tree in 1792, a custom followed till today, though now the state government is the sole owner of all sandalwood trees. At the turn of the nineteenth century, Mysore produced an excess of sandalwood. Buying manufactured soap was just becoming fashionable, so King Nalvadi Krishnaraja Wodeyar, the Maharaja of Mysore, ingeniously decided to use sandalwood in soaps. In 1916 he established a Government Soap Factory.

Mysore Sandal Soap instantly appealed to the Indian upper classes as the most fragrant soap in the market, even though it was first sold in the form of cakes without packaging. Later, in the 1960s, a butter-paper packaging (with the mythological animal Sharabha, a creature with the body of a lion and the head of an elephant on it) was adopted. This unmistakable green and red packaging continues to this day.

For a long time sandalwood was inexpensive, but then the demand rose internationally and it was over-harvested. Felling was banned by the Government of India in the 1930s (along with musk, another prized perfumery ingredient from the Himalayan deer), and export of sandalwood dwindled to a bare minimum. In 1950, 4000 tonnes of heartwood were produced, but by 1990 this had dwindled to half.

Exceptional sandalwood oil comes from trees aged around fifty to seventy-five years. After its ban, old trees that existed on private plantations became so highly valued that it led to the creation of well-organized sandalwood smuggling outfits. The government tried to crack down on them but it took eleven years to capture Veerappan, the leader of the country's biggest sandalwood smuggling racket – who owned about two-thirds of the total sandalwood jungle area.

Since 2004, the government has once again taken control of sandalwood plantations and the Karnataka Soaps and Detergents Limited that inherited the Mysore Government Soap Factory is cultivating over 60,000 saplings a year to afforest sandalwood. Meanwhile, the demand for the Mysore Sandal Soap is so high that until the trees flourish again, they have had to resort to younger wood from the neighbouring states of Tamil Nadu, Kerala and also Australia. Its provenance might have changed for the time being, but to its millions of fans the Mysore Sandal Soap is still the most important part of their daily bath.

NANO

The world's cheapest smart car

Date of Origin: 2009
Material: Metal, plastic, rubber

The Tata Nano is a compact, four-passenger vehicle with a length of just 3.1 metres! At one lakh Rupees ($2,000), it is the world's cheapest car. Nano's concept and price point trumps ostentation, making it singular compared to high-end cars like the Daimler's mini-car Smart. Its 623 cc, cleverly rear-mounted two-cylinder engine with a length of just 3.1 metres maximizes interior space, and the cables that traditionally run in front from engine to accelerators now function from the back. This single innovation has resulted in thirty-four patents making the Nano a singular example of frugal design.

When Tata Motors announced their plans in 2003 to build the world's cheapest car, the reaction was endless at home and abroad. Sceptics saw nothing more than a box on wheels. In fact, the initial design brief at the Engineering Research Centre in the Pune factory of Tata Motors did not depict the Nano as a car. The concept was to create a people-carrier. The design team questioned the relevance of doors, considered plastic instead of metal, and wondered if a low-powered engine would suffice.

Mock-ups of the Nano included a vinyl-door device with plastic windows and a cloth roof. Media gossip had by now started questioning the 'car-ness' of the Nano, to which the company stated that the Nano 'is not a car with plastic curtains or no roof – it's a real car'.

When the first Nano hit the country's still-developing roads, it was greeted with cheers nationwide. Henry Ford's Model T, the first people's car, and the Fiat 500, one of Europe's all-time favourite cars, both share a rear engine similar to the Nano's. But at the time these two cars were released, almost a century ago, they did not have to pass the global challenge of climate change. The Nano's fuel economy of 4.55l/100km makes it a relative gas-sipper, and it only produces 101g/km of CO_2 emission; the Smart emits 112g/km and the Mercedes Benz C-class 155g/km.

The March 2009 launch of the snub-nosed Nano was the product of six years of tests. Spare but functional in detail, the Nano has one instead of two screen wipers; has no power steering but an AC option, a simple interior, no airbags and plastic bumpers. Its boot is tight: at a max of 130 litres, it limits luggage to a weekend's supply of necessities. So when Nano, the country's latest – and most controversial – car hit the roads on 23 March 2009 it became the most talked about car around the globe. It is the most seductive car especially for a family of four seeking to upgrade from a two-wheeler.

NATHNI

An ornament for the nose

Date of Origin: Unknown
Material: Gold, silver, titanium

Nose rings and pins are believed to have spread all over the world from India. But traditionally they have been worn not just in the country but also all over Central Asia. It's only modern India that continues wearing it, because even for the hippest, coolest and most cosmopolitan of Indian women, the nose accessory represents her link to tradition and an expression of her Indian identity.

Whether it's in one or both sides of the nose or as is sometimes the case, the septum too, the nose ornament when in the left was the sign of a married woman. Their shape, form and motifs differed from the ring to studs or hooks depending upon the region. But they have never been a part of traditional Indian jewellery culture and their widespread use came only during the Mughal period where it spread through the country, Indian women well aware that it could only enhance their beauty. Amongst all Indian jewellery the nose ring is the most secular without a deep religious or social significance. The hippies introduced it to the West where celebrities like Katy Perry and Christina Aguilera set to wearing it as part of all their outfits. And to conquer the attention of the world, it is Lady Gaga who has gone a step further and made the septum ring popular too.

Traditionally nose rings and pins were mostly in silver and gold. But now there are a mesmerizing variety of unusual materials like acrylic plastic piercings, glass spirals, titanium studs, hand carved horn particularly for the septum and of course platinum.

Even for the woman who does not wear a nose ornament habitually every day, they do form a part of her wedding jewellery. Amongst such a vast variety of nose rings to choose from it's quite a task to find the most suitable. And that is where one turns to Bollywood. Since the film *Jodha Akbar* was released in 2008, nose ring fashions have been universally united into that one large hoop that actress Aishwarya Rai who played Princess Jodha Bai wore in the film. This is the nose ring of choice now, a wondrous object of sculpture, decoration and identity.

NEHRU JACKET

A politician's favourite jacket

Date of Origin: 1940s, New Delhi
Material: Wool, cotton

Indian fashion has often found creative solutions to wardrobe conundrums. The Nehru jacket is an iconic example of this: it is a shorter version of the smart yet slightly stifling sherwani – a long seventeenth-century coat. The Nehru jacket freed the legs and looked handsome with a pair of gabardine trousers. This fusion of fashion perfectly suited the East-meets-West elegance of the 1940s. Its hip-length structured body resembled the suit jacket but its upright collar was distinctly Indian. This combination put the jacket on the global fashion map.

The man responsible for this jacket was India's first prime minister, Jawaharlal Nehru. There are many stories around the origin of Nehru's idea. On a trip back from Beijing, he reportedly acquired a Mandarin-collared women's jacket and asked his tailor to replicate it so that men (himself included) could wear it. Nehru had the jacket made in various lengths and designs to suit the occasion. Designer Ritu Kumar attributes Nehru's style preference to the heavy-brocade achkan coats worn by the Awadhi royalty in the seventeenth and eighteenth centuries. Nehru swapped the expensive brocade for the khadi fabric that was adopted by India during its struggle for independence from the British. Whatever its origins, it became synonymous with his personal style and the Nehru jacket gradually became associated with formal dressing. Nehru liked to pair a knee-length version of the jacket with tight white churidar pants, and a rose in his buttonhole. This ensemble was his trademark.

Internationally, the 1960s' London threw the austere, centuries-old tailored dark suits off the fashion radar and embraced colourful lapels, collars and ties, known as the Peacock Revolution. The Beatles too began sporting the Nehru jacket after their tryst with India and Ravi Shankar. Classy shops around Piccadilly Circus purveyed the design to fashion iconoclasts,it thus became a must among stylish Brits.

The Nehru jacket could be hip length or longer, and worn with jeans, flared trousers or tuxedo pants. In 1968, After Six, America's leading tuxedo company featured a Nehru jacket in their advertisement. American entertainers chose it for their public appearances. Sammy Davis Jr, with a few hundred jackets in his wardrobe, is perhaps the most famous wearer of this jacket. Stylists have adapted the Nehru jacket for celluloid. Bond villains in *Dr No* and *Tomorrow Never Dies* wore it but it has a more apocalyptic silhouette when worn long by characters Neo and Severus Snape in *Matrix* and *Harry Potter* series respectively.

A staple in every discerning man's wardrobe, men's coats have moved back to formal styles or to sporty-chic styles. On the contrary, 'Antwerp six' designer Dries Van Noten and 'master-cutter' Yohji Yamamoto continue to be inspired by the Nehru jacket and have at least one in most collections. The Nehru jacket is now an unofficial preference of all the diplomats and parliamentarians at any formal gathering in India or abroad. The classic black and white photographs of the jacket taken by photographer Dayanita Singh in 2000 evoke their regal presence and underscore Nehru's timelessness.

NETI POT

A pot with an ergonomic spout designed for yoga therapies

Date of Origin: 500 BCE
Material: Metal, Plastic

For practitioners of yoga, purification or cleansing is an important part of their daily practice. Flushing the inner passages of the body is believed to give a clearer view of the world. The neti pot assists in this cleansing ritual and is one of the very few 'props' used in yoga. It is designed to assist a yoga technique of nasal irrigation called neti, which helps promote a healthy sinus and nasal passage that are considered gateways to human spiritual transformation. As the practice of yoga was adopted worldwide, the neti pot too became global and is now easily available in drugstores around the world. Oprah Winfrey introduced one on her show, as being more effective than medicines to cure sinus.

Cleansing and purification of the colon, intestines and nose forms Shatakarma, one of the eight paths to complete yoga. The practise of any one of these eight stimulates the other seven. Neti leads to cleaner breathing, fresher eyes and therefore higher energy, creativity and inner peace. It gently massages the sinus and also works as a good preventive measure for chronic sinusitis and nasal symptoms.

Neti uses two types of props: a pot with a spout to pour water in the nose and a string to insert from one nostril into the other. Using the neti pot is the easier one of the two and even the uninitiated can become adept at it in a few sessions because it is designed to fit in the nostril such that water can flow smoothly from one to the other.

Smooth practice of this exercise requires stability of the body, being seated on the floor or standing, and pouring sterilized and lukewarm water with rock salt into one nostril (tap water cannot be used as it has bacteria which, unlike the stomach, the nose cannot kill). The water then goes behind the nasal septum and exits through the other nostril. Salt helps maintain the same ph level as the body. With the pot it is easy to keep the head tipped forward so that the water does not spill into the throat. This process is repeated through the other nostril. The nose is then dried rapidly by forcefully blowing a couple of times.

Neti is considered most effective when practised in the morning, usually at the beginning or end of yoga practices. The process is repeated once a month initially and eventually daily. Traditionally Indian yoga practitioners used a special brass pot with a narrow nozzle – its flat base fitted perfectly in one's palm, and its spout inside the nostril. This pot, in time, came to be called the neti pot. The spread of yoga all over the world led to the neti pot being produced in ceramic, porcelain and other lead-free materials. While those adept can also practise neti with a regular lota or even the palm, the neti pot lends ease and comfort to the process. Practitioners say that sometimes it takes two–three neti pots before one finds the right fit.

NIRANJAN

A ceremonial lamp that lights up every prayer service

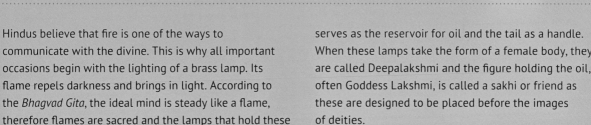

Date of Origin: Unknown
Material: Brass

Hindus believe that fire is one of the ways to communicate with the divine. This is why all important occasions begin with the lighting of a brass lamp. Its flame repels darkness and brings in light. According to the *Bhagvad Gita*, the ideal mind is steady like a flame, therefore flames are sacred and the lamps that hold these flames are important objects in the daily life of Hindus. Whether earthen or metal, they are a testament to a unique design tradition that turns symbolism first into art and then into useful objects.

So much so, that amongst the thirty-six different craftsmen employed by the Jagannath Temple in Puri, Odisha, there is one group dedicated solely to lamp-making, specializing in brass and bell-metal ware. The most imposing pillar lamps are placed at the entrance of the temple and the sanctum sanctorum to illuminate the path of the worshipper. The largest of these hold five hundred flames; lit in the evening, these lamps are left burning till the oil in them is fully spent.

Smaller votive or aarti lamps are made for the inner sanctums, an area accessible only to the priests. Designed to be held in the hand, they have a handle with many small cups to hold oil and often have different motifs such as swans or peacocks – the most favoured being peacock, because they are believed to carry the human soul to heaven and be the bridge from darkness to light. The lamp is designed so that the bird's body serves as the reservoir for oil and the tail as a handle. When these lamps take the form of a female body, they are called Deepalakshmi and the figure holding the oil, often Goddess Lakshmi, is called a sakhi or friend as these are designed to be placed before the images of deities.

While the pillar and votive lamps made in metal are imposing and ceremonial, the oldest form of lamp, the diya, is smaller and made of clay. These earthen diyas are made by potters who hand-mould them into small, shallow bowls. Cotton wicks are placed in oil at the pointed edge that holds the flame. These earthen lamps might be the most humble of all lamps but they have been found amongst clay objects at the excavation sites of the Indus Valley Civilization.

The most common in India are the standing brass lamps, called *sukunda*. They are simple with four or five wicks, and light both homes and temples. A tray holds recesses called devas for the wicks that is joined to a slender brass stick on a heavy round base. The five wicks represent earth, water, air, fire, and aether that are considered a manifestation of the divine, human and earthly. Sometimes there is a figure on top of a lamp. When it's Garuda, the celestial bird of Vishnu, the lamp is meant for the worship of Vishnu. Left burning even when the devotee is not present, the lamp is believed to make up for his absence.

NOTE MALA
A garland of bank notes for the groom

Date of Origin: Unknown
Material: Bank notes, thread

To the unknowing eye, there is nothing quirkier than a bridegroom in an impeccable suit with a matching tie, a beautiful red turban with gold trimming and a big garland of real bank notes. This pomp is an integral part of Punjabi wedding finery though by no means restricted only to Punjab. In fact it has been lavishly embraced by most of north India.

Kinari Bazaar in the heart of old Delhi is where the patu'a work is done. These are craftspeople or jewellers who specialise in threading ornaments. Most famous for making tassels, they also use these techniques to make the rakhi, the sehra worn by bridegrooms and also simple threads tied around the torso or the wrist during special occasions. They are the unsung jewellers responsible for the most Indian of necklace closings, the knotted-ball that slides up and down the necklace on the back to adjust its length.[21]

While creating ornaments that are for festivities particularly garlands, the yarn of choice is either precious, if finances permit or in any case metallic. This is what is used in the rakhi, the money garland and also the sehra. This garland of appropriately chosen bank notes is meant to make him look worthy while pitching into the wedding expenses.

In 2016, as a result of the latest demonetisation, which in itself has quite a long tradition in the country since 1946, when the country's five hundred and one thousand rupee bank notes were stripped as legal forms of payment, amongst those that were hit were the money garland makers. In the cash strapped days starting in November of that year, people thronged to old Delhi and other parts of the country where the garland makers practise their craft hoping to exchange their larger denominations of the smaller denominations from the garland makers. Alas the garland industry was the worst hit as no cash meant no garlands.

Its origins are baffling but India is the world's only major culture that worships Laxmi, the goddess of wealth so openly. The visual impact of the money garland is definitely north Indian baroque at its finest. While the tradition of the money garland is fading, the patu'a continues to work on demand as and when summoned by jewellers or in the homes of individuals, where they can spread a piece of red or white cloth to work on and a few tools of trade that helps them to braid, twist, wrap, and knot with yarn.[22]

PAAN AUR PAAN DAAN

A shared palate of betel nut and leaves

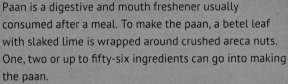

Date of Origin: 1700 CE
Material: Betel leaf, nut, silver

Paan is a digestive and mouth freshener usually consumed after a meal. To make the paan, a betel leaf with slaked lime is wrapped around crushed areca nuts. One, two or up to fifty-six ingredients can go into making the paan.

Paan is meant to be shared, not just materially but also with the senses. In miniature paintings paan-stained lips denoted sensuality. Lovers' trysts always accompanied paan served from a paan daan. In a typical painting, a couple is shown enjoying a bida, another name for the paan, resting on simple round large plates with a cover and smaller dishes inside for the leaves and accompaniments. There are a number of compartments and containers inside the paan daan and since paan dans are custom made, each one is unique.

A paan dan is used to store these ingredients. As seating was often done on the floor without furniture or objects, the paan dan and the hookah were the two objects that garnered most attention while designing as they were made with the sole purpose of sharing.

Paanch-pati or chaupala are the boxes that hold five of the most important ingredients used in a paan: areca, cardamoms, cloves, nutmeg and anis. Fresh, moist leaves are stocked in separate, often elaborately carved, silver boxes. The fillings could be in one box or have a separate box of their own. Sometimes small round containers joined at the hinge called chunal were designed to carry just the lime. A full set consisted of up to sixteen containers and included a spittoon called the peek-dan. Shaped like elaborate brass vases, they were used to spit and were so elegant that they became objects of collections.

Paan was shared in a way similar to tea during the tea ceremony in Japan. Each ingredient could have its own dish for serving, such as a plate in the form of a plantain leaf designed just to offer betel leaves. This added to the elegance of sharing. Paan bidas were often presented in silver cones made of filigree.

Patna, Varanasi, Kolkata, Hyderabad and Lucknow are all important centres of paan. Japanese lacquer, ivory and sandalwood paan dans were some of the preferred materials used in their design. Each city employed its traditional crafts. The sumptuousness of the paan service reached its peak in the eighteenth century when the paan daan became one of the many gifts exchanged amongst the ruling elite.

शिक्षित बेकाराने

धंदा स्वयंरोजगार

असा वाहनचालकांची सोय झाली
आहे. हा व्यवसाय अत्यंत फायदेशीर
असल्यामुळे यासाठी बरोडा बँकने

... दि. २४ (वार्ताहर)

...वाडा येथे नुकताच सरपंच
...गावकर यांच्या हस्ते कार-
...शिंग ...रचे उद्घाटन
...ले. या ...ग सेंटरचे
...मोद रेडकर, वडील धोंडू
...डकर, प्रितम शेटगावकर,
...गावकर, गुरुनाथ खोत,
...रिक विष्णु मोरजकर
...ते.

...धोंडू रे...यांनी नारळ
...शर पंप स्टार्ट करून कार-
...ग मशीन चालू केले. मोरजी
...ष्ट्या अग्रेसर असल्याने
... दुचाकींची संख्या खूप
... वाहना... मोरजी बाहेर
...ने धुवाची ...गत होती.
...थील या वॉशिंग सेंटरमुळे

प्रमोद रेडकर यांना आर्थिक साहाय्य
दिले आ... एका सुशिक्षित युवकाने
स्वतःचा रोजगार सुरू केल्यामुळे इतर
युवकांनी अशा विविध व्यवसायांकडे
स्वयंरोजगार म्हणून बघण्याची स्फूर्ती
नक्कीच मिळेल, असे उद्गार उद्घाटन
सोहळ्यावेळी सरपंच धनंजय
शेटगावकर यांनी काढले. या वेळी
मोरजी परिसरातील कार व्यावसायिक
मोठ्या संख्येने उपस्थित होते.

मोरजी येथील मोरजाई
मंदिराकडून श्री सत्पुरुष मंदिराकडे
जाणाऱ्या रस्त्यावर श्री सिद्धिविनायक
कार-बाईक वॉशिंग सेंटर काररत आहे.
अधिक माहितीसाठी प्रमोद रेडकर
यांच्याशी संपर्क साधावा.

क्रीडा संघटनांनी माहिती अधिकारी नेमावा

पणजी : दि. २४ (प्रतिनिधी)

राज्यातील ...क्रीडा संघटनांनी
माहिती अधिकारी नेमावे
मागणी माहिती हक्क...
आधारित ६ व्य...
आली.

गोवा ...
इंटरनॅशनल सेंट...
केलेल्या 'माहि...
सुप्रशासन' या ...
झाली. या वेळ...
क्रीडा प्राधिकरण...
क्रीडा संघट...
कोयद्यांतर्गत...
नेमण्यास स...
करण्यात आली...
मुख्यमंत्री, क्रीड...
असावी. असा...
उपाध्यक्ष रुई फ...
बर्वे यांनी मांड...

या वेळी ...अध्यक्ष नंदिनी
सहाय यांनीही मार्गदर्शन केले.

एकल गाय...

हणजूण | दि. २४ (वार्ताहर)

...विकासात
...सते. घरी,
...रीत सर्व
...तातून एक
...तून ...लांच्या
...नळ ...तूनच पुढे
...गायक तयार होतात.
...लांनी अशा स्पर्धातून
...व्हावे, असे अ...
...स्कूबर्ट को...
...ण येथे...ले
...हायस्कूलू...
...य सोलो गाय...
...वितरण समारंभ...
स्कूबर्ट कोटा...
सिक्रेट हा...
श्रीकांत ...
...था...

...ल परिसरातील शेतीचे नुकसान...

...२४ (वा...फिर)

...यवाट पाहिली. केप...च्या
...च्या शेतकऱ्यांनी विरोध दर्शविला
होता.

शेतकरी विनोडकर यांना अवघीच
शेतजमीन अ...ल्याने त्यांनी विरोध
केला.

...ह...च्या ओहोळाच्या आसपास
...माती टाकल्याने विनोडकर झाली
पंचायत ...मामलेदार कार्यालयात तक्रार
दाखल केली होती व तक्रारीनुसार
तलाठ्याने अहवाल तयार करून
...मलेदारांना पाठविला.

...वसाळ्यात या ओ...
...या वापर पाणी वाहून ज...
होती, ...र अन्य दिवसात त्याचा वापर

...क्षत्रातील गिरकरवाडा
...करवाड्यावरील मुख्य
...असलेल्या ओहोळाचा
...साळा ...ख्ता पायवाट
...र होतो, त्यामुळे
...सानी भोसावी लागत
... संताप व्यक्त होत आहे.
...डबावरून पूर्वी फक्त
... गिरकरवाडा दांडो
...होते, त्या
...राल लागायची.

वाहून जाण्यासाठी यो...
जातात असेही ...
वास्तविक रस्ता ...साठी जमीन
संपादन झालीच नाही; परंतु जबरदस्तीने
दगड-माती टाकून लागवडीखालील
शेतजमीन व शेतीचे नुकसान केल्याचे
मात्र दिसते आहे.

नाल्याच्या दोन्ही बाजू बंद केल्याने
पाणी जाण्यास वाटच नाही. परिणामी
शेतीचे नुकसान होईल व त्यास
जबाबदार कोण, असा सवाल शेतकरी
विनोडकर यांनी ...ताना केला.

...मामलेदार, उपजिल्हाधिकारी
आदींनी ...ल न्याय द्यावा व
प्रत्यक्ष भेट देऊन परिस्थितीची पाहणी

...न न...

...ी गर...

फाद...

खान...

उपा...

स्पर्धे...
येथी...
होत्या...
सेंट...

...न...

वाळपई दि. २४ (प्र...

गोव्यात क्रीडा क्षेत्र...धान्य
देण्याची गरज अस... क्रीडा...
उन्नती होण्यासाठी ...डा...
केले पाहिजे. ...नंतर ...त
चांगले क्रीडापटू निर्माण ...ही, असे
मत क्रीडामंत्री रमेश त...कर यांनी
वाळपई येथील प्रशिक्षण केंद्रात क्रीडा
साहित्य वितरण व ठाणे-डोंगुली
येथील क्रीडा संकु...चे उद्घाटन
कार्यक्रमात प्रमुख ... म्हणून
बोलताना व्यक्त कर...

होऊ...
भागा...
पाहि...
तवड...
विद्या...
पाही...
व्ही.ए...
संचा...

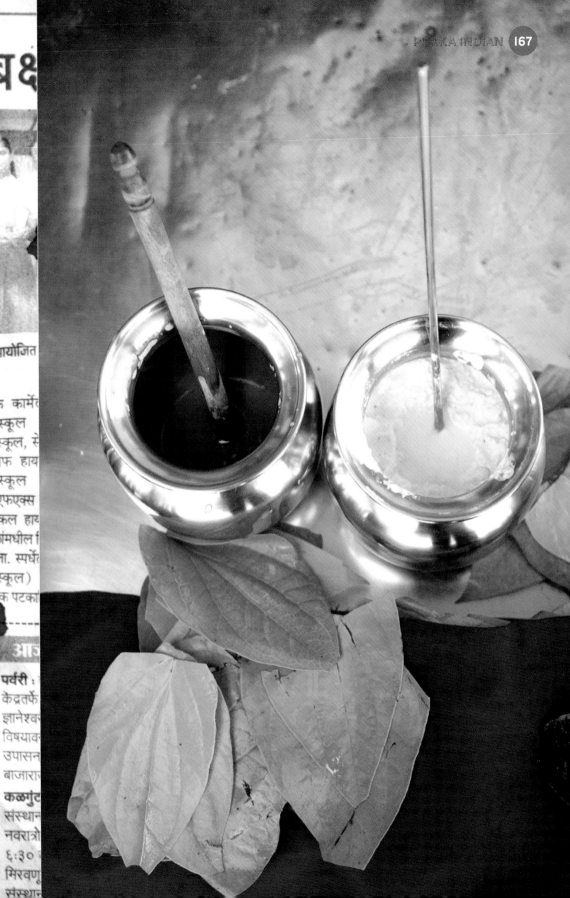

PASHMINA SHAWL

The finest woven wool product ever designed

Date of Origin: 1700 CE, Leh, Srinagar
Material: Fine wool

The pashmina shawl is a status symbol all over the world today. The diamond-shaped squares, a result of the fine tapestry technique called tapestry-twill, that cover its surface are a mark of the finest woven woolen product ever designed. It was the Mughal Emperor Jahangir, a noted patron of the arts, whose obsession with its design first turned it into a craze in the seventeenth century. He deemed pashmina exclusive only for himself and a chosen few to whom he offered them as gifts.

The pashmina has become more prized than any other shawl around the world because it is believed to be the warmest, softest and finest. Srinagar in the Kashmir valley is the centre for pashmina shawls. This is where the soft ones are woven but higher up in the mountains around the city of Leh is where the Pashm goat grazes and provides the wool for the shawls. The temperature here is one of the coldest in the world going down to minus thirty degree or more. Pashm is the down closest to the animal's skin that insulates it from the cold. Down is the finest fibre and pashmina uses yarn from the longest of these fibres. It is removed from the goat's body by hand-combing in stages so the animal stays protected during the receding winter months from June to August. The fistfuls collected at a time are then hand-spun into a yarn.

Colour even though mostly neutral is a defining trait of the pashmina shawls. Ecru, which is the closest to the colour of the goat, is the hallmark of the pure Indian pashmina. White is prized because it can then be coloured in different hues. The pinks, greens, yellows and most other multi-coloured pastel ones are actually a Nepalese invention using a mix of pashmina and silk, a combination that offers tourists instant gratification at a cheaper cost than the pure Indian pashmina. They don't have the distinct tapestry weave of the pashmina and are loosely referred to as cashmere, a mispronunciation of the region of Kashmir.

There is often confusion between cashmere and pashmina wools. Both refer to the same wool but there is a difference in the length of the fiber. Cashmere is not hand woven but mechanized, weaving short-stapled yarn of 3.5 cm or less. Pashmina weavers use a handloom and a longer staple of 5 cm in a finer yarn thus making it a superior wool that is harder to find, making the pashmina the finest wool product in the world.

But pashmina shawls are not only characterized by their wool but also the uniqueness of each of the steps that go into making them; the weaving, dyeing and even its repair after its use is painstakingly done by specialized artisans. This rhythm of beauty spun by the artisans creates a product that has been referred to as woven poetry in texts dedicated to the pashmina shawl.

PATANG

Kite, a symbol of independence

Date of Origin: Unknown
Material: Paper, bamboo strips

The Indian fighter kites are the 'Porsche' of all kites. They are light and strong. The design allows reactivity in movement up, down, left and right. The dihedral angle formed by its wings makes it stable. This makes the Indian kite different from any other single-string kite as it can maneuver against the wind.

The multicoloured Indian kites or 'patangs' were part of the collection of American designers Charles and Ray Eames. They used them as decoration in their architectural projects. For them, kites were not just objects to fly; they were a study in the efficiency of design. Indian kites were a part of this because they are made with the lightest of building materials arranged in a playful construction. These were the architectural qualities that the designers tried to embody in their work.

Amongst all kite-flying countries, Indian kites look the simplest because they are designed to 'fight', and can fly up to 2000 feet. They follow one basic form – small squares made of fine coloured paper kept in shape with two bamboo sticks, a straight one that is longitudinal and the other one that joins both the sides in an arc. This arc is crucial as it increases the flexibility of the kite. This way the patang resists wind pressure and lifts faster.

Patangs of the same size participate in competitions. The game is to fly high and then to maintain supremacy by cutting the threads of other kites. The thread too is designed for fight. The spool called the 'firki' holds the 'manja' or kite thread, which is made of cotton but covered with glass powder and rice starch so that it cuts sharply.

There is a technique to the fighting. On a fine spring day, tossing a coin decides the place where the kites will be launched from, a terrace or the ground. Knotting the manja to launch the kite and then stabilizing it in the sky is what every kite flyer learns. To cut and win, the best position is to hold the string between the thumb and the index finger letting the rope slide easily.

Enemy kites attack first from below to cut the thread. And this is where the agility of the patang is in full display. Thwarting means to swing the kite and escape swiftly. So the rope is tugged and then released. Tugs on the string lift the kite and moves it away from the attacking string.

Patangs are light and resistant. They fly high and react with agility because they can bear strong wind pressures necessary to gain speed in the fight. This makes the Indian kites the lightest, swiftest, albeit smallest of the kites in the world.

PATILA
A multi-purpose metal pot

Date of Origin: 8000 BCE
Material: Stainless steel, other metals

In the pre-Vedic period three pots signifying heaven, earth and a mythological underworld were part of rituals. These pots were used to boil milk for offerings and consisted of deep dishes with rims in different sizes. This was a prototype of the patila that is now used in kitchens. Their primary function today is still to boil so their form remains the same – a deep dish in metal with good heat conductivity and a rim that helps hold the pot. If kitchen utensils were to form a landscape, patilas would be as ubiquitous as trees.

In the early Vedic period, as temples grew larger, worshippers proliferated and large numbers of people had to be served food inside the temples. This is when many varieties of patilas came into being; deep large-mouthed vessels used for cooking foods for both divinities and devotees. Stirrers and ladles for use in these pots came into existence in the later Vedic period.

Patilas are made without handles and necessitate the most ingenious of kitchen tools, the pakads. These grips are in the shape of scissors but with a straight arm and a curved one that fits around the rim, the best and the only way to hook and lift a boiling pot. This is useful because a detachable handle that is perpendicular to the walls of the pot would require a strong grip whereas a pakad hooks the rim and therefore lifting requires much less effort. Patilas come in many sizes and a pakad is the unique solution for handling all of them. Hooking a pot with a pakad is easier compared to the weight felt with a typical cantilevered handle.

In today's India, patilas are made of heat-sensitive materials like aluminium and stainless steel and come in all sizes, such as those with a seven-inch diameter meant for a four-person household to cauldrons used to cook for over two hundred people in wedding banquets. Halwais cannot make mithais or desserts without condensing milk in a patila.

Patilas are handmade, two sheets of aluminium are welded together, one for the bottom and the other for the sides. Using only one sheet would mean the aluminium would have to be stretched, and the thickness of the metal would become uneven, affecting the heat dispersion. This is how the patila has been made since its inception.

Patilas made of brass or copper are made in the same way and were a part of a bride's dowry. A third variety called Ganga-Jamuni is made of brass and copper fused together.[23] These coloured metals are used for both cooking and serving. They have resale value and so are kept safe and polished vigorously with coconut husk, mud and tamarind. While these find pride of place in the kitchen, the workhorse of every home stays the humble aluminium or stainless steel patila because without it, it would be difficult to boil milk or rice.

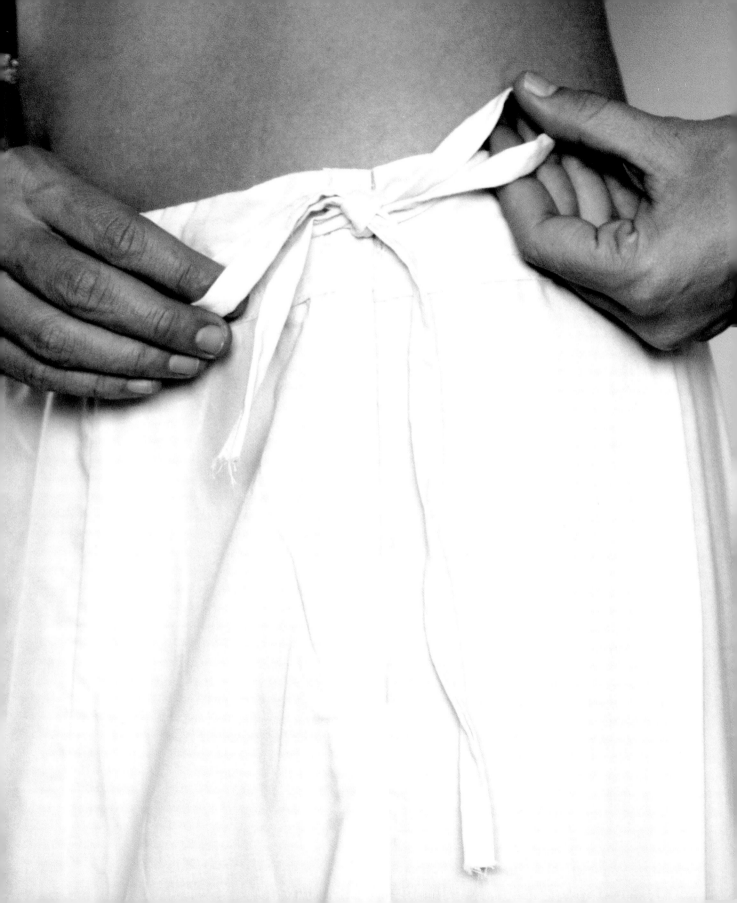

PETTICOAT

A skirt-like garment worn under the sari

Date of Origin: Unknown
Material: Cotton, polyester, string, lace

The petticoat is responsible for giving the sari a unified image throughout the country, as the sari can be worn easily and does not slip. The wearing of the petticoat or generally a garment under the sari started in Rajput and Mughal western regions of the country due to growing conservatism in the seventeenth century, so the earlier version of the sari was only knotted around the waist like the lungi and with one separate drape on the shoulder, actually becoming one garment worn with a blouse and a petticoat called the *tehposh*.

Initially it was simple, but slowly it acquired details of embroidery and lace, a distinct inspiration from imported clothes. Tehposh made of silk and Chantilly lace was not entirely uncommon as a dowry item of upper-class Rajasthani women. The petticoats were made long on purpose and the sari kept in a very light material so that its beauty below would be apparent. It was even considered coquettish. The nefa or the girdle around the petticoat was sometimes made of another cloth or colour and a nada or drawstring passed through it to tie it. The simple ones that are worn today were actually reserved for the poorest. Even those who could not afford the beautiful ones had the fall inside lined in silk.

The initial designs of the petticoats took their inspiration from the ghagras or lehengas that had been worn for centuries. Petticoat was also the name that the English gave to the ghagra, such as what the Jesuit priest Father Fallon says while translating a common north Indian song about a woman wearing a ghagra–choli going to collect water from the well and being teased by young boys: 'Oh! Oh! What mischief dire the mice have wrought; they have destroyed the fair one's petticoat'. Women in Europe had started wearing it since the fifteenth century as skirts under their skirts to give them warmth and also to give volume to the skirts, quite the opposite function to what it was meant to do when adopted under a sari which was more to secure it.

So whereas the petticoat gave way to trousers and skirts in Europe, in India as more and more women joined the work force the sari, the blouse and the petticoat ensured that the sari stayed modern. But one size certainly does not fit all. And the simple drawstring can scrunch up the petticoat around the waist, making one apprehensive about one's silhouette. And that's where the 'fish cut' petticoat comes in. A brilliant idea: the mermaid-shaped bias cut around the waist keeps excess fabric out. It's the best and most subtle support that the sari could ever have.

PHOOL MALA

A flower garland to celebrate every moment in life

Date of Origin: Unknown
Material: Cotton string, flowers, leaves

Flower garlands are worn to mark important moments in life, like marriage and death and also examinations, the starting of a new business or a house. In the ancient era, even something as important as choosing a husband was expressed through a simple garland of white flowers. The Mahabharata gives a detailed account of this custom of swayamvara where a girl chooses a groom amongst many suitors by garlanding him with a special string of white flowers. Even today, any Indian marriage ceremony includes exchanging of garlands between the bride and the groom.

According to the Kamasutra, a good wife is proficient in sixty-four art forms. One of them is the art of gathering and arranging flowers and stringing them to make garlands for the hair. But today garlands are woven in the flower market and this is where the flowers are freshest. Stringing flowers is similar to folding paper for origami. Both require deftness of fingers and speed. Jasmine buds are tied together with a fine cotton string in a long strand. White cotton threads are then twisted into adjustable loops where the flowers are placed and the thread tightened. The whole process takes just a few minutes. Simple strands or multiple ones, only the freshest flowers are used as ornaments in the hair and as

necklaces, bracelets and anklets during weddings. The thickness of the garland can go from a single string for the hair to more than a dozen reserved for deities. They are then dispatched immediately nationwide and also to Indian communities in the Middle East and Southeast Asia. Fragrant flowers like rose, jasmine and tuberose are the most valued for garlands, used in combination with frangipani, lotus and champak.

The choice of these flowers is not by chance. According to Indian mythology, Kama, the god of love, shoots arrows that have been dipped in five flowers that represent one of each of the five senses used in making love: the gigantic swallow-wort, jasmine, mango, saffron, and champak.[24] The gigantic swallow-wort is traditionally what was used for the mangalsutra necklace. Jasmine and champak remain the most popular for garlands as flowers are not just decorative, they are also used for their scent. But despite their fragrant presence, fresh flower garlands are ephemeral and so their beauty is immortalized in metal jewellery. The champakali necklace, a classic Indian design, is an ode to the champa garland. Through a string of silver pieces shaped like the petals of a champa flower, it recreates the beauty of a fresh garland strung around the neck that will never wear out or be discarded.

PLANTER'S CHAIR
A lounging 'lazy' chair

Date of Origin: 1800 CE
Material: Hardwood, cane

The exact origins of these chairs are unknown, but the British administration is believed to have imported it to India from Sri Lanka where they were widely used on the tea plantations. These low, reclining, easy-chairs are over a metre long and characterized by the arm rests that pivot to create a lounging position and a leg rest for the feet. Their design in wood with a cane weaving in a continuous section for the back and seat makes them much more comfortable than the sofa in humid climate.

The best position for relief in summer is raised legs. As heat dilates the blood vessels, reclining the body and raising them to the level of the heart helps in returning the blood. The chair is credited to have evolved from nineteenth-century offices in the country, where British administrators would raise their legs and often recline using the morha or the rattan stool as an ottoman paired with bamboo chairs.[25] This need for raising the feet while seated was combined in the planter's chair in the later nineteenth century and was exported as 'Indian chairs' to British colonies around the world in Southeast Asia, Africa and the West Indies.

The chairs still remain an integral part of the landscape on tea plantations. Bungalows set atop hills with spacious verandas are often dotted throughout their length with planter's chairs. On plantations they still denote hierarchy, as only managers and their assistants traditionally own and use them to unwind after daily rounds in the gardens. In the rest of the country such as in Mumbai, they have become collector's furniture and can be found in antique markets where they are uninhibitedly referred to as the 'Bombay fornicator'.

The planter's chair travelled to other hot and humid parts of the world such as the islands of the Caribbean, Africa and North America. It's in Mexico where they underwent a further change and even adopted a new identity where they became part of the design movement called 'Mexicanismo'. The arms were shortened as there was no need to recline for hours to observe plantations, and the rattan was replaced by *vaquetta* leather, a material common in these cattle-growing cultures. These chairs, called 'Butaque', became a favourite of artists and architects such as Luis Barragan and contemporary ones like Riccardo Legoretta who introduced them into the homes of the rich and famous in Hollywood and other parts of America. These 'lazy chairs' as they are still known in many parts of the world continue to grace porches and living rooms.

PRESSURE COOKER

A chef's best friend for fast cooking

Date of Origin: 1959, Bombay
Material: Metal, rubber

When the pressure cooker entered Indian homes in the 1950s, it completely altered the pattern of life in a typical middle-class home. Housewives and mothers now saved tremendous amounts of cooking time, of course, but also soaking time (for rice or dals) – the pressure cooker streamlined the use of a vast array of cooking pots into just one, as rice, dal and vegetables could be cooked in one go. The aroma of steam cooking of food combined with the pressure cooker's piercing whistle is still the sound of a secure, happy home. But most of all, it freed women from being slaves to the stove.

Housewives became so adept at pressure cooking that by the 1980s they were even baking cakes and experimenting with new recipes like stews. The famous Indian chef and food writer, Tarla Dalal, devoted an entire book to recipes prepared in the pressure cooker; she writes in her introduction, 'no matter what time of the year, when you are hungry, go for the "new fast foods" such as stews and easy-to-cook vegetable dishes, which can be whipped up promptly using a pressure cooker". Soups and stews have since then become a winter staple in homes.

When steel idli pathrams came to the north Indian market, they were made specially to fit inside a pressure cooker. The convenience of being able to make idlis almost instantly in an idli maker is what helped the tradition of the idli disperse itself far and wide from south India where it came from.

Pressure cooking also gained popularity in the West because it was healthier and faster. It was convenient for Indian cooking because its sealed lid allowed increased temperature and pressure, cutting down on cooking time for hard substances, and spices could be added too. Cooking hard Indian staples like rice and dal together, twice a day requires time, and steamers were never an Indian favourite because they didn't use oil, a necessity in perfuming food with spices.

In the following decades, use of the pressure cooker became widespread and can be directly linked to the large number of women entering the workforce in big cities. For now they could cook lunch for their families before leaving home in the mornings, which took only about twenty minutes instead of sixty. A further, typical 'Indian' innovation was the big nine-litre pressure cooker, which came with separate containers to boil rice, dal and chana all at once in separate holders that fit one on top of the other inside. Quantity was important too. In the early stages of use of the pressure cooker there were two favourite brands, TTK and Hawkins. They looked identical but Hawkins had a flat lid and TTK a curved one. The latter was preferred because the curved lid made it possible to fit even more rice and dal inside.

So the pressure cooker though designed elsewhere is one of the most important objects in India as it completely remodelled life at home as well as work, while adding a completely new culinary repertoire to the Indian diet.

PUNKHA

A hand-held fan for respite during power cuts

Date of Origin: Unknown, wall fixtures 1800 CE
Material: Bamboo, cloth, wood

The punkha was the only way to battle Indian summers. Paintings attest that when it first debuted in the late eighteenth century, it consisted of ornate drapery that hung from a wooden beam and a pulley system with a rope pulled by a servant dedicated to this task, which ensured a constant breeze.

British India became addicted to this mechanism and by the early nineteenth century, all rooms in houses including verandahs and churches were equipped with this device. The iron rings used in suspending these are still found in buildings of the period all over the country. The valance textiles ranged from simple ones to heavy brocaded materials often made to specifications to complement the interiors.[26] The 'punkha-puller' (known as PP) became an occupation and was on the payroll of the Indian Administrative Services and the Indian Armed Forces until the mid-1980s when coolers and air conditioners were introduced.

Just like in the rest of the world India too has a rich variety of hand-held fans; they do not open accordion-like as in Japan and Spain because they are made differently. The most unique hand-held fan in the country is the rotating punkha: it is designed to create breeze 360 degrees – it is organic, and is a beautiful object. It is made like the other fans of the country: a bamboo stick that serves as an axis for the hand to hold is attached to a fan fashioned from large leaves such as the dried palm-leaf or woven matting. Then a simple bamboo tube is slipped on to this stick that serves as a grip and pivot on which the fan rotates, providing relief not just to the one holding the fan but to all those around. When there is a power cut, this punkha is what makes the heat bearable.

In the early twentieth century, household electricity replaced punkhas with pedestal fans. This fan fulfilled people's aspirations for a comfortable life. The pedestal fan adopted varietals like the table fan and the ceiling fan that continued to be called the punkha. It is ubiquitous today, the most popular being from the company Khaitan. Khaitan fans were part of the essential dowry that a woman received as part of her wedding gifts. But during the interminable hours of load-shedding during the summer months, the hand fan re-appears in the guise of a saviour.

ROYAL ENFIELD

A cult vintage motorcycle for contemporary riding

Date of Origin: 1950, Chennai
Material: Metal, rubber, plastic, rexin

'Made like a gun, goes like a bullet' was the motto of the Enfield Cycle Company (ECC) when established in Worcestershire, England, in 1893. This is where the Royal Enfield Bullet motorcycle got its name.

In 1949, Enfield's tooling was sent to Madras Motors, India, where it was assembled and sold to the Indian army. The Indian military had agreed to acquire eight hundred 350 cc Bullets only if they were manufactured indigenously, so gradually by 1955 all components of the motorcycle were made in Madras. At this time, the Bullet was considered the most powerful, stable and rugged military machine. In 1970, the parent company in Worcestershire closed production as its counterpart in India flourished.

Over the years, the Royal Enfield Bullet, popularized by the army and police, became a machine of desire for young people rather than duty for the soldiers. In many parts of the country, the Royal Enfield was the preferred first bike for motorcycle enthusiasts. And till date more than half of Bullet riders are under 30 years old. But, despite its popularity for five decades, by the late 1990s this powerful machine was about to die a sputtering death. It was considered unreliable and a gas guzzler, and lost its market share to lighter, inexpensive Japanese sport commuter bikes.

So to combat this, in 2001, Enfield launched the Electra and repositioned itself as a leisure bike rather than a military machine: the seating was made more comfortable, indicators added, mudguards remodelled and with its new palette of colours and an electric start, it became a biking enthusiasts' motorbike. With its 350 cc engine, it was the world's only entry-level 'vintage classic'. (Vintage classic is a term given to a selection of ten of the world's finest classic cruiser bikes. Royal Enfield shares this with Harley Davidson and the Indian Chief.) After the Electra, Enfield decided to ride foreign roads with a model that had a new engine to comply with international markets. A design unit was set up within the company dedicated to this new model.

The latest Bullet named Classic C-5 was launched in 2010. It embodies the spirit of the 1951 motorcycle, the most vintage of Royal Enfield bikes with its sprung saddle and spray-painted frame. The nakedness of the bike, the classic graphics of the dial and most importantly the long-stroke 'beat' that makes a Bullet recognizable in any part of the world are a continuity of the Enfield tradition. The new five-speed gear box, redesigned engine, switches and clutch make it modern and emissions compliant.

So, while the new Enfield is now running on the roads of Paris and London, it still maintains the satisfaction of a true vintage, but with a more reliable and smooth driving experience than the previous versions. And despite the many bikes in the market launched over the last few years, nothing compares to straddling a Royal Enfield Bullet with its solid piston sound forging through rural countryside or the city at dawn.

RUPEE I

Indian currency that has always captured the zeitgeist of the moment

Date of Origin: 1992
Material: Cupronickel

Amongst all the denominations of coins, the one Rupee coin is the most symbolic. A wallet is incomplete as a gift if it does not contain it. Even cash gifts are propitiously rounded off such as Rs 1001 or even Rs 100,001. India was one of the first countries in the world to issue coins. It was the Afghan ruler Sher Shah Suri who introduced the Rupee in 1538 and called it the rupayya. Throughout the history of India until the 1960s, the one Rupee was the most circulated of all coins. Sher Shah's rupayya was made of silver and weighed 178 grams with a standard pattern: the place of mint, the date of issue and the ruling sovereign. By the fourteenth century, every passing ruler had found a method of dominion through the country's unit currency of which the one Rupee was the most prevalent.

Over the centuries, the rupayya has reflected the zeitgeist. The Mughals used design as an expression of elegance and employed zodiac signs, portraits, poems and refined calligraphy necessitating a canvas. So, the one rupee coins of this era were amongst the largest in the world. But even then the largely independent hundred or so princely states of India minted their own coins. When the British crown started annexing these states in 1825, the indigenous images prevalent till then were removed and a single unified Rupee was created. It had a portrait of the monarch William III. The one Rupee coin was initially made of silver, but when the price of silver rose at the end of World War II the government decided to introduce nickel Rupee in 1947.

It was evident that India would recreate its indigenous identity through its coins after it became a republic on 26 January 1950. Hereafter, the one Rupee coin underwent many changes. Its most memorable version is the one with a large numeral '1' flanked by two stalks of wheat and the value written in English and Hindi with the year of its issue. Introduced in 1992 in cupro-nickel, a light material, it was designed to represent progress and prosperity. When the price of cupro-nickel rose, the government introduced a new coin in stainless steel – that was the lightest Indian one Rupee coin ever issued, weighing just 4.85 grams.

In 2010, the government decided to create a symbol for the Rupee. Designed by a young architecture graduate from Mumbai, D. Udaya Kumar, whose interest in Indian scripts and typography led him to combine both the Devanagari and the Latin scripts with a double horizontal line at the top, making it distinctive enough to represent the Indian Rupee and yet fit into the design of the international currencies. So, just as the one Rupee is symbolic in daily life, in history too, despite its many faces, it has always signified an auspicious continuation with designs that have been a reflection of India's state of mind.

SAROTA
A betel-nut crusher with the sharpest blade

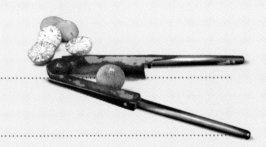

Date of Origin: Unknown
Material: Metal

The sarota or the betel nut crusher can be compared to the samurai's sword; a combination of the sharpest blade set into a hilt that is intricately carved. The blade of the Indian betel nut crusher made of 'wootz' steel is in fact as legendary as the samurai sword. It is set into a highly decorated frame used to crack betel nuts to chew with betel leaf. The use of the betel nut crusher is so prevalent around the country that there isn't one particular style of blade or grip that gives a unifying identity to its design. The length is the same, around six inches long, but there are hundreds and thousands of designs and no two are the same.

The sarota was prized because it was made of wootz, a particularly strong steel. Its manufacture started a thousand years before steel was used for weaponry in the rest of the world. The Indian wootz blade was famous and was one of the many objects traded from the country in the first millennium BC to Greece and Rome. They were prized for their hardness.

The blade is forged from ingots obtained from the alloy of iron with carbon. It is first heated at a high temperature. This turns soft high carbon steel to harder low carbon steel. Plunging the hot blade into the trunk of a banana tree and finally cooling it hardens it further.

This lengthy process is crucial for the tough edges that are a prerequisite for wootz blades.

While the sarota is an article used mostly in a home environment, the other famous use for this steel was the Damascus swords and daggers that were the most prized possessions of Mughal aristocracy. Miniature paintings of the period from the fifteenth century onwards often paint both the sarota and the dagger, present even during meetings between lovers.

The sarota is almost a product of alchemy used to crack betel nuts. Betel nuts themselves are charged with symbolism that serves as inspiration for the design of the body of the cutter. Radha and Krishna as lovers sharing the betel nut is a common theme in miniature paintings, because the betel nut and leaf represent the union of male and female.

Birds, horses, celestial nymphs, gods, and goddesses are all used to give form to the grip surrounding the blade. Mostly made of metals like brass, steel, bronze and also woods like bamboo from the Andaman and Nicobar islands, the prized ones are even studded with glass and precious stones. Betel nut crushers exist around the world but the ones made in India are unique because they are a combination of great metallurgy with mythology.

SARI

The six-yard-long piece of cloth that drapes the body beautifully

Date of Origin: Late 19th century, Calcutta, now Kolkata
Material: Cotton, silk, chiffon, other fabrics

Stitched clothes were considered impure during rituals in ancient India. The sari, in its drape, follows this Hindu philosophy of purity but combines it with a sense of beauty and practical climatic concerns by draping woven cloth loosely over the torso and the legs. Hieun Tsang who travelled in India from 629 CE in his work *Si-Yu-Ki* recorded that both men and women wore two pieces of seamless draped cloth. This tradition is still prevalent in many parts of the country like in Kerala and the Northeastern states. It is difficult to rationalize why or when the sari became a one-piece garment. But the most common version of the sari as we know is a one-piece cloth, a 1.25 metre wide and five to nine metres in length. The sari remains one of the world's oldest national dresses worn even today. It has only one form but as many identities as the women who wear it.

A 108 variations of the sari drape have been identified, varying from region to region, such as in Maharashtra where it was tucked between the legs making it easier for women to work in the fields or in Coorg where wearing the pleats at the back freed the gait compared to a more rigid drape without a pleat. Despite the variations, modern India chose to follow a unified style that was propagated by the vibrant Tagore-led intelligentsia in Bengal in the last quarter of the nineteenth century, who in turn borrowed it from the cosmopolitan Parsis of Bombay.

At that time Victorian conservatism considered a sari with an almost bare torso unacceptable in public. So a blouse and a petticoat were added to cover the bust and hide the legs. This period saw intense social changes, and many women started experimenting, travelling and assimilating drapes from around the country. So the most convenient way became the way it is worn today, a sari with a fall stitched in for strength, a petticoat for the skirt and a blouse as a top. This became respectable outdoor wear, as stitched clothes are structured to mimic the body whereas the sari adapts to it.

The sari needs the body to give it shape, until then it is just a very large cleverly conceived canvas of colour, texture, embroidery and weave, woven in identifiable sections. The border extends all around the sari but a change of pattern signifies either the pallu (thrown over the shoulder) or in some cases the pleats in front. Modernism in the 1950s brought in imported sensual fabrics like transparent georgette and silk-voile that did not follow this pattern as they were often a block of monochromatic colour, five yards cut from a bale of cloth. Further innovations included such unconventional experiments such as the stitched sari that proved to be unpopular. The sari might be the simplest piece of fabric, but as a garment it is a deep reflection of the wearer's identity. The gesture of draping it shall always remain an enigma to the non-sari wearer.

SARI BLOUSE
A blouse that completes a sari

Date of Origin: Between 1800 – 1850 CE, Calcutta
Material: Silk, cotton

Blouses changed the way the sari was worn. Amitav Ghosh in his novel *The Glass Palace* says that it was a missionary's wife who invented the sari blouse and the petticoat. Till then women considered blouses unnecessary as the sari was draped over the shoulder covering the breasts. It was in Westernized urban centres like Bombay and Lucknow in the late nineteenth century that the blouse was first spotted, worn matching with the sari. The evolution in their design is also the reason why the sari too has always stayed contemporary.

In India, because stitched cloth was considered impure, the sari was worn without its matching blouse for centuries. But British administrators and Christian clergy like Abbe Du Bois were startled by this dress code, which to them seemed immoral. The first to be seen sporting a sari blouse were the women of the upper strata of the society in Bengal. The blouses were stitched to be as close as possible to the skin so that the appearance of cloth was minimal. This was a new form of sensuality and a blouse with the sari was considered respectable outdoor wear. Victorian modesty dictated that the first generations of blouses, often full-sleeved and stitched long to cover the navel.

While there are many designs for the blouse today, two basic designs are preferred. Tailors call them the 'plain blouse' and the 'choli cut'. The plain blouse has a large scooped neck and back. Four darts on either side of the torso give shape to the bodice. The choli cut

is similar but with broader shoulders, a looser fit and fewer darts. Indian women since the eleventh century had worn cholis, blouses, with stitched skirts or ghagras. While the blouse is a more recent addition to the wardrobe and is often made in simple cotton, cholis have more embellishments such as piped edges to accompany special occasions.

Blouses have seen many versions of sleeves as they became fashion statements. Long sleeves and puffed sleeves were in vogue among the upper-middle class in Bengal during the early twentieth century, while the lower classes were usually seen wearing half sleeves or sleeveless ones. Blouses and saris so far were bought separately and then matched. In time, the blouse became a canvas for weavers who started weaving it as an extension of the sari on one piece of cloth, which could be turned into a blouse.

In the 1920s and 1930s, cinema started having an impact on fashion. Blouses became sleeveless and sexy or extravagant with frills. The saris worn to go along with them were sheer, often in imported French georgette. From here onwards the blouse became accepted, inseparable from the sari and very trendy. They also helped translate the sari into formal office wear. This is unique in a world that often just clings to its traditional forms of dressing or relegates it only to ceremonial occasions. The sari blouse keeps the tradition of the sari relevant and contemporary.

SEVNAZHI

Making sev or fried savouries, a childhood favourite

Date of Origin: 1400 CE, Goa
Material: Brass

India's obsession with comfort food starts with the savoury snacks consumed at all times of the day, often for breakfast and always with tea. The country offers infinite varieties, the tastiest of which are prepared at home with a device called a sevanazhi, a manual press with multiple cutter disks. The sevanazhi is used for making idiappam or string hoppers in southern India, and sevai, bhujia and murukku savouries in the north. Made of brass, it resembles a manual pasta maker, but is smaller, with a strong base and a screw handle to squeeze the paste into shape.

Its lineage is impossible to trace but pressing and shaping food with an aid rather than the hand is unusual in India. Papads, chapatis, dosas and jalebis are all hand kneaded or hand poured. The Portuguese in Goa brought with them a press for making angel's hair, a dish made of fine strands of egg yolk. But whether this is the ancestor of the sevanazhi or not remains a mystery. Incidentally, Goa today is a centre for crafting brass sevanazhis.

The press itself is small and has a cylindrical shape 6–7 centimetres in diameter. This circular base is ridged to tightly hold a perforated disc plate through which the dough is squeezed. These perforations come in many designs: a large round one, star shape ones from where the paste is poured into a snail form, tiny ones of two millimetres, three-hole ones that are around 5 millimetres in diameter, a large slit across the centre that makes flat savouries, and many other shapes that lend infinite variety.

Preparation of the paste is simple – water with ground rice is used for string hoppers and gram flour for the sevai. This paste is poured into the shape from the top, after which a screw device pushes it through the perforated discs. Traditionally sevanazhis were made of either brass or wood, but new materials such as aluminium, steel and plastic, that are no longer manual, have also made their way into the market. The brass ones, however, are the most beautiful and one of the heaviest objects in the kitchen. In many homes there is a preferred savoury shape for everyday, but for special occasions the abundance of shapes signals a celebratory mood.

SHATRANJ
India's favourite board game

Date of Origin: Before 500 CE
Material: Wood, plastic, ebony, ivory, lac, sandalwood

The game of chess originated in India. Akin to the duel in the medieval world, chess was a method of resolving conflicts. The game was favoured by royalty who commissioned sumptuous chess boards often offering them as gifts and outdoing each other's ingenuity of design. For the princes of Rajasthan, the largest chess boards were not just board games, they were elements of architecture. Terraces were inlaid with white and pink sandstone that served as the checkerboard. The pieces were people in the service of the ruler who wore head-dresses to represent kings, queens and horses and moved in steps as ordered by the players. These massive chess terraces, such as the one at Jaipur's Jal Mahal, were often built at points where the sunset could be watched while playing the game. Such extreme design for recreational purpose is unusual in most cultures. Even chessboards that were not human in scale adopted unique elements of design.

Since the 1600s, the trading city of Vishakhapatnam on the east coast of India had a tradition of making furniture of wood and ebony inlaid with ivory. This technique of inlay work, due to its contrasting colours, was used in chessboards often meant for the international market. They were veneered with ivory and tortoise shell. Pieces could be stocked within the board that was inlaid at the bottom with sandalwood on which one could also play another game, backgammon. These book-shaped boards are singular because they could be folded and clutched in the palm of the hand and carried. This design enabled a game of chess or backgammon at any time and any place accompanying hunting parties or summer retreats.[27]

Chess is played not through single, linear movements but through combinations of movements. To play it well one needs to simultaneously connect the different movements of the pieces. This system of synchronicity originated in India on a board called the Chaturanga that literally means four limbs.

Chaturanga travelled to Persia and was called Shatranj that was played with different rules than in India. It spread through Persia, Spain and all of Europe, acquiring a larger board and more pieces. The rules followed in India varied slightly from European ones. Besides elaborate chess boards, many manoeuvers known as the 'Indian defences' were born in India. They were characterized by movements that were porous but good for creating immediate opportunities. The Olympic player Mir Sultan Khan of Punjab was a sensation in Europe in the early 1930s bringing this 'Indian-style manoeuvering' as one of the important grand master styles in the world. In the 1930s, it won him the British chess championships thrice.

The game of chess is a true representation of India. The design of the chessboard reflected India's lifestyle that was characterized by movement such as during change of seasons. Indian-style manoeuvering reflects Indian psychology too, where actions for a series of quick short-term gains are often preferred to a longer term vision.

SHIRODHARA MASSAGE EQUIPMENT
Neuroligical healing

Date of Origin: Around 500 CE
Material: Clay, copper, brass, hardwood

Shirodhara has a similar effect as meditation on the human brain. Firstly it alleviates excessive pressure on the adrenalin glands by relaxing the nervous system and it also soothes and smoothens brain waves. The impact it has on the mind is so tremendous that it is not even considered a massage but more of a therapy. As its name suggests (Shiro meaning head and dhara meaning stream), it consists of pouring oil down the forehead from above and sustaining this flow from half an hour to around an hour to reduce the vata or the 'wind' from the mind, which is the result of sustained stimulation of the senses and brain activity.

This neurological healing would be hard to practise without the special equipment it entails. Firstly a pot positioned over the forehead with a hole at the bottom that can release a continuous steady stream of warm oil. This sensation of oil flowing on the forehead is what provokes a healing response in the brain by igniting an oxygen intake.

As the pot is positioned around 15 centimetres above the recipient's forehead, the therapist holds it and deftly moves it horizontally or vertically, either just at the tip of the eyebrows from ear to ear or vertically along the head; a third movement is a focus on just the third eye. While the simplest versions consist of only a pot with a hole that is hand guided, the shirodhara equipment is actually quite extensive. It will have a shirodhara stand, a copper or brass vessel, both with healing qualities, with a control valve, and electric oil pump that pumps the oil continuously into the vessel above the head.

Even though technology has intervened in the process, in India where touch and therefore manual systems are given more importance than automated systems, the shirodhara equipment consists of a similar stand usually in hardwood and a pot. But the oil is heated and poured into the vessel by hand using traditional brass vessels called the kindi that is a pitcher with a nozzle used to pour the oil and the uruli that is used to heat the oil. Thus time seems to have never crept in between traditional and modern India, and the human touch that is true to Ayurveda stays put.

SHUTTLECOCK

The game bird

Date of Origin: 1877, Karachi
Material: Goose or duck feathers, cork, leather

The shuttlecock is the only flying object that is made of the very material that makes birds fly – feathers. Sixteen overlapping feathers, usually of goose or duck, are arranged on a cork in an aerodynamic design. When hit with a racket the shuttlecock shoots swiftly into the sky, its feathers facing up and when it loses speed it lands gently, feathers first. The feathers give the shuttlecocks a much higher top speed, so its trajectory is different than the balls used in most racket sports. They also create a drag that causes the shuttlecock to decelerate more rapidly than a ball. The challenge of the game is to predict precisely where the shuttlecock is going to land, challenging because of the various speeds of the shuttlecocks.

It's a sport that many Indians particularly women excel at. Like archery and shooting it requires concentration, making it a sport that is easy to train as an individual, rather than in a group. This excellence is closely linked to the use of the shuttlecock in this sport. It is unknown when or where the first shuttlecocks were made. But the modern game of badminton is believed to have come from the Indian game called Poona. Its rules were laid out for the first time in 1877 in Karachi.

Today shuttlecocks are machine-made in China but continue to be hand-made in India. In Jadurberia village near Kolkata, which is one of the many villages in the shuttlecock-making belt of the country, each feather is cleaned thoroughly and dried in the sun following which the edges are neatly trimmed to align into a cork that holds them together. Each shuttlecock takes a few hours to make.

Since its origin, badminton was the preferred game of the administration. Even today most residential areas that belong to the government have a badminton court. This makes badminton both social and physical activity. For some followers of the game, like the writer Saskia Jain, the shuttlecock is a metaphor for life in the country, as the tension between two people playing badminton or their conflict makes a narrative. This is playfully reflected in the song 'Dhal Gaya Din' from the 1970 Hindi movie *Humjoli*, where a man and woman play badminton on a date. The beat of the song is rhythmic to the racket hitting the shuttlecock. They dance waiting for their turn to return the shot. Hilarious as the choreography of the song is, it is also a telling account of the shuttlecock and the game of badminton and its deep association with India.

SIL BATTA
A flat mortar-and-pestle grinder

Date of Origin: Unknown
Material: Stone

The origin of sil battas can be traced to the Tittiriya Samhita, a guide to rituals written during the Vedic period. It lists ten objects that an Indian kitchen must have. This includes a large stone slab called drasad used to crush or grind the soma creeper with the help of a smaller stone called upala placed on the drasad. In a history of over three and a half millennia the sil batta has been used continuously almost every day.

The heaviness of the bottom slab makes it immobile while the top slab shaped like a brick, just large enough to clutch in the palm of both the hands, serves as the weight. The mortar and pestle and the sil batta, however, are two different objects. The sil batta pulverises to a fine paste using flicks of the hand. The movement of the hand is straight rather than circular as in the mortar and pestle so the surface area for grinding is larger. This is also a practical solution to a mortar and pestle because it is flat and can be neatly put away after use. This method of grinding using a a flat stone is found in Andean cuisine too, where is it called batán and is used to crush grains such as quinoa but more importantly and similar to India, to crush chillies and tomatoes to make a hot sauce.

While pounding can be done without much concentration, one ingredient at a time, sil batta is about multi-tasking. The early mashing of garlic, just like in cooking to make the flavour bloom, then the tossing of chillies and coriander together so they blend consistently, and finally the mixing of all the ingredients on its flat surface, and the preparation of the chutney is complete. Indian cuisine uses at least five to six spices that are crushed at home for every meal and the sil batta helps with this. Even when not in use the serrated surface of the platform combined with the smoothness of the stone is awe-inspiring. Stately and beautiful, they look like archeological relics but continue to be used in kitchens everyday, because who needs a cumbersome mixer that is expensive and consumes precious resources when the sil batta works just fine.

SINTEX TANK

Water storage tank for all of India

Date of Origin: 1979
Material: Virgin and food grade polythylene plastic

Rain is a real challenge in some parts of India. Fatehpur Sikri was abandoned in the twelfth century because of drought. In the West rain comes rarely but in the East it comes in floods. Only forty-five per cent of urban homes and one-fourth of rural homes have access to tap water. So storage of water and its transportation to deficient areas makes overhead water storage tanks essential. This is why the strong, lightweight, portable, easy-to-maintain, Sintex water tank has found many takers. They might be black and bulky but nevertheless India has formed a relationship with them as water is what maintains the city's chain of life.

Sintex tanks are truly innovative borrowing plastic technology not from the water industry but from a completely disconnected textile industry. Sintex was originally a textile company with a small plastics unit acquired in the early 1970s when the textile business needed card cans (used for cleaning fibre), for which the company had imported plastic rotational moulding technology. This idea of plastics in the textile industry did not work out. But the company did not stop there, thinking laterally to see if the rusty overhead water tanks could be replaced with new plastic ones that the company could build. This is where the name of the triple-layer water tanks came from – 'Sin' from the sintering process of fusing plastics together and 'tex' from textiles, which is what the plastic technology was

initially for. The company's 'one-piece-ready plastic tank' was exhibited for the first time at the ChemTech exhibition in Bombay in 1975. Around that time there was a cement and steel crunch in the country, and as overhead tanks polluted the water it led to the debut in 1979 of Sintex water tanks, made from virgin and food grade polyethylene.

They were lightweight, durable and foolproof, and the black colour was chosen to block the sun's harmful UV rays. Consulting architects shunned the idea as the tanks looked ugly on top of buildings, nevertheless, it was the functionality of clean, safe and leak-proof material that won people over. Though now Sintex water tanks are available in white too.

Sintex tanks are not only on the top of most buildings in the country but also on the ground, on trucks, tractors and construction sites. They were made portable for people who added floors to their houses. They were also expandable so that two or more tanks could be joined with a pipe to increase the storage capacity. Today a city without these tanks is doomed to failure as 60 per cent of the water in India is supplied by Sintex tanks which store 12,000 million tones of water at any given moment. The design of these tanks has won many awards, and is a plastic superbrand that touches the lives of everybody because it stores water: an element without which life ceases to exist.

SOOP

Winnows are used for sifting rice and wheat husks

Date of Origin: Unknown
Material: Bamboo

Winnows or winnowing fans are used to sort grain. A few fistfuls of lentils are placed in the deeper part of the winnow and flung in the air. When the grain catches the bamboo, the clear, heavier grain stays on the deeper end and the lighter waste ends up on the shallow side and can be removed with a flick of the hand. A simpler method would be just lifting the fan into the air where the lighter chaff blows away with the wind. Winnows are a product of agricultural technology of all societies that cultivate grain, but in India, every region, state and tribe has created its unique style and shape of winnow. And while each is made with ingenuity, all use the widely available material of bamboo.

One of the major types of winnows has a broad shovel shape with a flat front and a scooped rear. Its uniqueness is in its curved shape yet high resistance, made possible by the flexibility and tensile strength innate in bamboo. The flexibility of the material allows it to be bent and fixed along the periphery of the curved form. The high tensile strength of the fibre allows it to carry heavy loads of grains. Its water-resistant nature makes it suitable for humid regions.

Winnows can be curved or trapezoidal and the bamboo-weaving varies with the width of the bamboo used. These shapes and weaves reflect a mastery of splitting different bamboo widths inherent in each species of bamboo. Of the 700 species grown worldwide, 136 grow in India. Each winnow is handmade and is slightly different in shape. One of the most unique winnow shapes is made in the Mon district in Nagaland. It has a scalene shape so that the longest arm can be used to pour grain after separating.[28]

All winnows are stark, simple and ingenious. Design however is far from the minds of the craftsmen who make them, but functionality too is not foremost on their minds. For them it's a habit, a simple and resourceful way of putting their bamboo-rich environment to good use.

SUMEET MIXER
The mixer-grinder that made cooking easy for everyone

Date of Origin: 1960s
Material: Metal, plastic

It is accepted today that the cornerstone of food preparation in India is the Sumeet mixer, loved for its versatility from beating eggs to grinding rice. No utensil dowry is complete without one because its range of blades blends, mixes and grinds just about everything from the grocer. More than the milkshakes that the company pamphlet suggests, in the South it's the traditional dishes like the idli and dosa batter; and in the North, it's the tomato puree and chutneys that makes the Sumeet mixer the engine of every kitchen. Most South Asian celebrity chefs have a personal mixer that they never travel without. The imported French Moulinex blenders or German Electrolux food processors brought as gifts from relatives living abroad can't compete with the Sumeet mixer.

Sumeet mixed, grated and whipped with multiple blades like all other blenders. But that is where the comparison ended. Its no-nonsense 750 watts meter with a speed of 19,000 rpm made it the most efficient non-professional grinder in the world. Even its body was designed for sheer power, a large block with a single dial and multiple jars of more than a litre for mixing. Grinding lentils needs this strength as does soaked rice for idlis. But the Sumeet did finer things too like dry (spices such as cinnamon sticks into a fine powder) and wet (chutneys with herbs and chillies) grinding.

Post-Independence 1950s' kitchens were equipped to compliment India's rapid urbanization and modernity. Indian kitchens embraced appliances, starting from the mixer, grinder, juicer, electrical oven and eventually the refrigerator (as companies like Kelvinator reduced prices, the refrigerator became affordable and a marker of social and economic status).

But while all these were just markers of modernity, Sumeet was a game changer. It was never aspirational but it replaced the millennials old twenty to thirty kilogramme stone-grinders and freed women from the drudgery of food preparation that was hard labour and time consuming. Food preparation couldn't have received more ingenuity than from its creators, Mr and Mrs Mathur, who declared, 'nobody ever put more into a grinder than we did!' Today most modern Indian kitchens, be it in New York or Bangkok, are equipped with one.

SURAHI / MATKA

A terracotta pot for storing and keeping water cool

Date of Origin: 1500–500 BCE
Material: Clay

Water in Indian culture is considered the elixir of life and signifies abundance. Thus, since its inception, the matka was as much an object of rituals as of domestic use, which is why it is still an important part of the country's daily life. The matka and the surahi are both one of the most sophisticated ways of storing water and at the same time keeping it cool. Their rounded shape holds the maximum quantity of water that can be carried by a single person. Porous clay allows adiabatic cooling that keeps it chilled.

The creation of the matka is related to the mythology of the surrounding rivers. Vedic Aryans from the proto-historic period celebrated the Ganges River, believed to come in abundance through a thousand streams imparting wealth and fertility, with a ritual offering of water. This was done through a pot made of ceramic with a hole at the bottom. Often this hole was elaborate, such as in the shape of a small carved head of a cow with water flowing through its mouth. Huen Tsang who travelled to India in the seventh century wrote about the storing of water at homes in earthen and porcelain jars.

The matka is made by potters all over the country. Amongst them, the Jagannath temple potters, as servants to the temple, have the most exalted status. The community believes to be assigned by Lord Vishnu himself to serve humanity and are therefore direct descendants of Rudrapala, Vishnu's own potter. They make pots for temple use. These pots are not just used for storing water but also cooking, serving and storing rice, yoghurt and other foods both for the divinities and worshippers. This tradition of using pots for other purposes other than storing ritual water is first recorded fairly recently in the seventeenth century, reflecting an adoption of royal court rituals in temples rather than just religious ones.

Even though their sizes might be different, potters have traditionally made the same designs of bellied jars for ages with water poured from them by tilting the mouth. Surahis have a slim neck and sometimes even handles and are thus used to serve water just as from a pitcher. Because of their weight when full, they are unwieldy for larger pots. So the potters of Puttur, a small town near Mangalore created a water filter from this traditional form. By adding taps and bases, they have made an object meant for ritual use into a user-friendly one meant for contemporary purpose. Matkas cooled water anyway but the potters of Puttur gave them a larger thermal insulation by placing a smaller pot within a larger one. The gap between the walls keeps the water even cooler. A lid and a tap are added for filling and dispensing with ease, thus giving a modern lease of life to a centuries-old object.

Thus the beauty of the matka lies in the fact that it remains a sacred object of rituals as well as a simple object used at home to store drinking water. Few objects around the world beat this versatility.

TABLA

Adding beats to every tune, this drum-like instrument is the timekeeper of music

Date of Origin: 1700 CE
Material: Goatskin, wood, clay, brass, rice and wheat starch

What the tabla does is give form to melody through beats, in other words it serves as a timekeeper in music. Melodies repeated over a set number of beats, forms the basis of music around the world. Clapping is the simplest way known to man to provide these beats. All musical cultures have transformed clapping into drums of which the tabla is just one form.

Classical music on the tabla is performed as a combination of three elements – two are the respective repertoires of the soloist and the tabla player, and the third is actually abstract, it is the intuitive rhythm born of the relationship between the two. The tabla player memorises his *thekas* or phrases and the soloist his lines. Together they create a rhythm that they shall have to maintain throughout the performance. None of them have the liberty to alter the rhythm of the piece. But while the soloist sticks to the composition, it's the tablaplayer who introduces a lot of variations and with it the joy and surprise within the set composition. Though vocalists are the prima donnas, it's the tabla player who through his/her understanding of the abstract *taal* or beats of the piece maintains rhythm in case the vocalist slips.

A tabla player has at his disposition two drums. The right hand drum is more cylindrical in shape and made of wood and the left hand drum is more scooped and made of clay or metal. Both hands are used to strike their goat-head top surfaces. Both the drums are set within interlaced leather cords that are used to tune the tabla by placing wooden blocks between the chords and the body of the drums. Moving this wooden block up or down alters the tension and therefore the sound emanating from the tabla. The surface of the drums can be struck to produce different resonance depending on whether they are struck closer to the centre or towards the edge. These variations produce the typical sound of the tabla that differs from light to complex. This is also the variation seen amongst the different schools of table-playing.

Common use of the tabla became prevalent fairly late in Indian music history. Siddhar Khan, sometimes also referred to as the inventor of tabla, and his descendants contributed majorly in establishing the tabla language and compositions in Delhi. It then spread to Lucknow where tabla-playing flourished as an accompaniment to Kathak dance.

All melodies emanate from common 'categories' that the tabla player recognizes, and therefore the player does not need to know every melody. The flexibility, though, is thanks to the existence of the third or abstract rhythm born out of the intuitive relationship between the player and the singer. It is this flexibility that has made tabla emerge from the position of an accompanying instrument, to an outstanding solo instrument in its own right.[29]

TANDOOR

The earthen oven that adds a smokey flavour to breads and tikkas

Date of Origin: 3500–2500 BCE
Material: Clay, coal

Indian cooking is synonymous with the tandoor. These clay ovens are not a recent phenomenon, they have been found in the remains of the ancient civilization of Kalibangan, Rajasthan. Houses in this early Harappan settlement (3500–2500 BC) typically had three to four rooms with a courtyard and tandoors placed in its northwest corner so that winds flowing from northeast to southwest would carry the smoke away from the house.

Since then till today, their basic design remains unchanged. The tandoor oven is made of pre-fired bricks of clay and grass that are stacked together in a round beehive shape around five feet high, that is open on the top with an air vent at the bottom for fire fed by charcoal. When the dough for flat bread is plastered on the wall, it sticks due to the moisture, and the intense heat created by its shape (close to 480 degrees centigrade) means that it takes under a minute for the bread to cook before it is scooped out and served.

For long, the tandoors were used particularly in Punjab to bake only tandoori rotis. The years immediately after post-Independence saw the flourishing of dhabas in Delhi and along the Grand Trunk route. These dhabas gave the tandoor an extended menu with slow-cooked black dal and meats such as chicken. The tandoor stays burning for hours so dishes can be cooked one after the other.

Contrary to the Harappan age, in contemporary India tandoors no longer are a part of cooking at homes because few people have courtyards. When Indian cuisine became popular in the 1970s in the UK, the 'tandoor' proliferated. Most of the thousand-odd Indian restaurants equipped themselves with the tandoor because like most traditional cooking the tandoor needs a few hours of pre-heating, and once warm the cooking happens very fast.

Tandoori cooking is always dry but every restaurant has its own paste of spices and herbs rubbed into the walls that give its dishes a characteristic taste. The naans and rotis are baked on its walls and the meats on skewers. Repeated use of the tandoor gives it a flavour. While tandoors were always charcoal-fired, recent variants such as gas tandoors are smokeless. They are also mobile with wheels and the clay pot comes in an outer steel casing. Hotels and restaurants replace charcoal with electricity sometimes.

The tandoor has always had an interested audience that includes restaurants, foodies, dhaba-goers and chefs of other cuisines such as Afghani and Iranian. It is believed that these are the countries where it came to India from, its origins in fact are believed to be even further in the Balkans. But the tandoor is synonymous with Indian food and no other cuisine. It is a very important fixture in any Indian restaurant kitchen around the world. It is versatile as it can be used as an oven and a grill. But beyond that it's the creativity in the flavours and dishes that Indian chefs have given to it that has made the tandoor the ambassador of Indian taste.

TATA ACE

Covering the last mile with this mini truck

Date of Origin: 2005, Maharashtra and Uttarakhand
Material: Metal, steel, rubber

Every country needs a smart way to travel the last mile. But not all have come up with an efficient way to do so. India is a nation of small business owners who needed a vehicle that was affordable, fuel efficient and could take on small loads for quick delivery. Trucks were used, but they are banned in cities during day time due to traffic congestion; so three-wheeler auto-rickshaws normally meant only for passengers were used for goods during the day. That is until the Tata Ace was designed. So, whereas the other famous 'small car' Nano had been designed working backwards from an ideal price of approximately $2,000, the Ace was designed keeping in mind the community that would drive it, so shape first and then cost effectiveness. The Ace was immensely successful as it offered this last-mile connectivity in an affordable and, importantly, a stylish manner, thereby changing the face of Indian commercial vehicles.

The Tata Ace is a small truck with a capacity of one ton, launched by Tata Motors in May 2005. The first Ace had a 700 cc engine which made it as powerful as the first Maruti Suzuki passenger car. To make it affordable, Tata Motors developed a water-cooled, twin-cylinder diesel engine. Even though the project was headed by an engineer from the same team as the Nano, its design process was unlike that of the world's cheapest car. Firstly, the design team consulted six hundred drivers and end users to create a design brief for themselves – a bottom-up approach. From these talks the designers learnt that whereas cargo movement between large cities such as from Delhi to Bombay happened on trucks, the transport between two smaller towns in the same state was on tractors that had a trailer attached. Smaller volume intra-city transport needed much smaller vehicles, which did not exist in the country.

With its small wheels, the Ace had the manoeuvrability of an auto-rickshaw but the comfort of a bigger, more stable vehicle. It could go faster at around 64 kmph and had a bigger cargo bed, close to two metres in length and width. The price of Rs 2 lakh made it more accessible to the middle and lower classes. Small-time business people now had a comfortable, stylish and more viable option to transport goods within the city.

Tata Motors did not expect that sales of thirty thousand vehicles in the first year would more than double in the following year. With time, the number of Ace vehicles on the road grew, and by 2012 it was the single-largest commercial vehicle in the country. The company launched its passenger variant called 'Magic' in June 2007. It was equally successful as it made inter-city transport more comfortable. Today, countless small-scale transporters and entrepreneurs benefit from the Ace. Its popularity runs much beyond roads and spills over into the driver's life. For example, in Tamil Nadu, Ace drivers find a bride easier than auto-rickshaw drivers.

VEENA
The oldest string instrument in Indian music

Date of Origin: 200 BCE
Material: Jackfruit wood, bell metal, brass, ivory, horn, steel

The veena has a particularly exalted status in Indian music because its chords can reach 'regions' that the human vocal chords cannot and that is how the veena became the most important accompanying instrument for Indian vocal music. The *Yajur Veda* states that for any rite to have an impact, two Brahmins play the veena while a third sings.[30]

The veena does not have a strict definition in Indian musical treatises. It is referred to any stringed instrument that could have one or more strings stretched on a long hollow body. In fact, frets and a bowl were not a must and are believed to be later additions when a gourd shape was attached near the neck to give balance and symmetry. The veena is often considered the oldest instrument in Indian music. Musically it produces a vast variety of sounds ranging from that of raindrops to surprising ones such as the sound of thunder.

Sarngadeva, the author of *Sangita Ratnakara*, says that each part of the veena represents a god and is therefore highly auspicious in its presence alone. The veneration of the veena started due to a combination of features. Most importantly, it is highly individual – sages like Narada and the Goddess Saraswati had their own veenas. Narada's veena was known as Mahati and the goddess Saraswati had a Kachapi veena, but the instrument was considered an object of great beauty and its rosewood body was embellished throughout. In the Saraswati veena, the bowl is at the lower end and forms a continuous part with the body albeit with a joint. Ekdandi veenas, considered the most perfect, are those where the neck, body and bowl form a single piece of wood without any joints. Veenas can be played vertically and horizontally both, which makes them unique as instruments, and every veena player has a distinguished playing style as his or her own vocal style.

The Rudra veena is linked to the north Indian dhrupad style of music with a slow development of the *rag* and an extended *alap*. The composition is long and meditative. The south Indian Saraswati veena is very rhythmical with an intensity quite in contrast to the north Indian one. The veena, is supposed to be the surest way to 'liberating' the mind, but it is a difficult instrument to play, with few proponents. It is this very feature that has led to its revival in the last few years with musicians like Nageshwara Rao taking it overseas and collaborating with Maurice Bejart or more recently Ustad Baharuddin Dagar exploring various contexts such as that of contemporary art.

Z-SHAPED PUMP

Wisdom in the shape of a petrol pump

Date of Origin: 1991
Material: Electronic box on top of mechanical pump chasis

Until the early 1990s, every petrol pump in India, a country with over hundred million cars, looked the same: boxy and unimaginative, with a display that was difficult to read for both the attendant and the driver. But as the Indian economy sped up, incomes increased and so did cars, pushing for the opening of more petrol pumps and greater competition. One way to attract customers was to look good. So Larsen & Toubro (L&T) designed the Z-line pump to give the frumpy old petrol pump a modern look – a sleek Z shape where the top bar which housed the display panel was electronic while the bottom bar remained mechanical. In India, petrol pumps had rarely been the subject of a careful design process. But because the Z-shaped pump was immediately so successful, it led to the modernization of thousands of petrol pumps across the country.

Until 1986, L&T was market leader in the pump sector and produced the bulk of the old pumps. But with competition L&T began to lose ground. So a project to design a 'new look' was taken up in 1989. The brief was a petrol pump that had to be strikingly different to create a visual impact in the market. It also had to be 25 per cent cheaper than the old model – a seemingly impossible task! But stringent design constraints are often the precursor to the most successful innovations. To fit the economics, the designers had to use the existing mechanical hydraulics design and the body had to be made of sheet metal, using existing manufacturing facilities. Furthermore, the pump's life span had to be a minimum of five years. But where L&T triumphed was in the aesthetics of the pump itself – while competitors brought in new models based on Western designs, L&T came up with an entirely new Z shape that not only caught the eye but also reduced sheet metal usage by 40 per cent.

In the new Z-shaped pump, the top horizontal arm contained a new electronic display driven by a microcomputer-based system. This gave the flexibility of having single, double or triple display models that showed consecutively, or simultaneously, the rate, quantity and price that the client had to pay. The crossed section of the Z joined the top part to the bottom unit containing the pump, filter and complete hydraulics.

The new shape of the pump emphasized by the Z-shape looked light and extremely modern. A line-up of these pumps gave a compact and efficient image. The lit electronic display on each pump not only made it look hi-tech but also made the reading transparent and user-friendly. Life was also easier for the attendants as the pumps opened on the top for quick maintenance. Small details like the glow panel around the indicator or the end indicator, setting the filling limit to the chosen money amount, made the whole experience transparent and petrol filling very easy.

NOTES

1. McHugh, James, *Sandalwood and Carrion: Smell in Indian Religion and Culture*, Oxford University Press, 2012, p. 130.

2. Ibid.

3. Untracht, Oppi, *Traditional Jewellery of India*, Thames & Hudson, 2008, p. 304.

4. Ibid.

5. Batuta, Ibn, *Voyages d'Ibn Batoutah, Texte Arabe (Société Asiatique)*, 4 vols, Paris, 1853.

6. Jaffer, Amin, *Furniture from British India and Ceylon*, V&A Publications, 2001, p. 109.

7. Untracht, *Traditional Jewellery of India*, p. 370.

8. Ibid., p. 152.

9. Dar, S.N., *Costumes of India and Pakistan: A Historical Study*, D.B. Taraporevala Sons & Co. Private Ltd., 1982, pp. 29–32, 49.

10. Mishra, Susheela, *Musical Heritage of Lucknow*, Harman Publishing House, 1991, p. 95.

11. Gautam, M.R., *The Musical Heritage of India*, Munshiram Manoharlal Publishing, 2001, pp. 14–20

12. Ranjan, Aditi, Ranjan, M.P. (editors), *Handmade in India: Crafts of India*, Mapin Publishing, 2009, W/GJ 418.

13. http://www.nid.edu/download/EamesIndiaReport.pdf

14. Ibid.

15. Patnaik, Devdutt, *Myth = Mithya: Decoding Hindu Mythology*, Penguin India, 2006.

16. Chattopadhyay, Kamaladevi, *The Glory of Indian Handicrafts*, Indian Book Company, 1976, p. 152.

17. Untracht, *Traditional Jewellery of India*, p. 217.

18. Ibid., p. 154

19. Jaffer, *Furniture from British India and Ceylon*, p. 68.

20. Ibid.

21. Untracht, *Traditional Jewellery of India*, p. 308.

22. Ibid.

23. Ranjan, *Handmade in India*, C/UT 174.

24. Untracht, *Traditional Jewellery of India*, p. 30.

25. Jaffer, *Furniture from British India and Ceylon*, pp. 68, 392.

26. Ibid., pp. 52–53.

27. Jaffer, *Furniture from British India and Ceylon*, pp. 162–64.

28. Ranjan, M.P., Iyer, Nilam, and Pandya, Ghanshaym, *Bamboo and Cane Crafts of Northeast India*, NID, 2004, p. 24.

29. Bagchee, Sandeep, *Nād: Understanding Music*, Eeshwar, 1998, pp. 58–63, 258–263.

30. Anantapadmanabhan, C.S., *The Veena*, Gana Vidya Bharti, 1954.

ACKNOWLEDGEMENTS

In the memory of Arushi

This book has taken many years to write and would have been impossible to complete alone.

I am particularly grateful to Radhika Jha who has read the draft many times, edited it and helped me find a voice. Despite our separation over thousands of kilometres living in Tokyo, Delhi and Beijing, she was always a phone call away.

Vrunda Pathare of Godrej Archives, who immediately opened up her Godrej almirahs and out came an incredible amount of carefully archived information on everything from the first lock to the first typewriter. Thanks also to Siddharth Lal and his team for sharing the design directions of Royal Enfield. The team at BPL TechnoVision, Sankara Netralaya and Abhijit Sansod at Studio ABD. Chanakya Oza shared his great grandfather's recipe and vision for Babuline gripe water. Radhika Piramal from VIP Industries and their design team led by Vasant Dewaji with Bijaya Mukherji and Navin Shetty who have such a commitment to design. Artist Priyanka Choudhary introduced me to spinning khadi which proved to be difficult beyond my imagination. Gita Ramesh shared with me the vast knowledge she and her family has of ayurveda. Jean-Marc Dameron painstakingly spent one entire summer reading various drafts and explaining the technical aspect of many of these objects, including adiabatic cooling and the workings of the human knee. Damion Mannings, Yann Le Garrec and Iris Touliatou have never used any of these products but treated the subject with as much love as I did by reading parts of the book, proving again that design has universal elements. The late Professor MP Ranjan and Dr Amin Jaffer were generous every time I approached them with ideas. Their own research served as inspiration for me throughout the book.

The photographer Shivani Gupta for being here, there and everywhere taking photographs at every opportunity of every product ever made in India. I am grateful for Shivani's respect of the continuity of tradition in the homes, of having the courage to shoot everyday life in India that might not always be lavish and placing products in anonymous settings. Aradhana Seth's understanding of structure and space and the constant presence of the human helped in defining this approach that enables the reader to grasp what lies at the heart of this book, a deep yearning to identify the fundamental features of Indian vernacular culture. Shivani's photographs are evocative, some like the money garland funny, and many of them touching and most importantly they are all Human. It is like a documentary, very real and very complex. With Shivani I wanted to keep this magic of the patina of time and authenticity of context rather than a romanticized imagination of objects. Thanks also to Munir Kabani who shared his photographs. Jagan Khursule assisted Shivani in making the photoshoots possible.

Of course my publishers Roli Books had the toughest job of making this quest of the vernacular interesting to the readers. For this I am grateful to both Priya Kapoor and Kapil Kapoor and their team. Their patience over the years has been unflinching.

A lot of these objects have been lovingly collected by people such as Priya and her team, who have carefully sourced many others.

I am thankful for the support of my family. My grandfather, Dr Vir Bahadur Singh, whose seminal work on the economy of India during the British Raj was fundamental in helping me understand the power of design during the Swadeshi movement. My mother and uncle shared his vast research with me over the years. My father had constructed a desert cooler when we were kids and there and then perhaps I became interested in the making of things. Then Kaveri, my sister, had the thankless task of calling up many of the companies who created these objects.

Most of these products are unassuming but they make what India is. With the help of all the people I mention above, I try to share the poetry of what makes India incredible.

FURTHER READING

Ahuja, Shyam, Ahuja, Meera, Maluste, Mridula, *Dhurrie: Flatwoven Rugs of India*, Antique Collectors Club, 1999.

Bhushan, Jamila Brij, *Indian Jewellery Ornaments and Decorative Designs*, D.B. Taraporevala Sons & Co. Private Ltd., Bombay, 1964.

Chattopadhyay, Kamaladevi, *Carpets and Floor Coverings of India*, All India Handicrafts Board, 1976.

Chishti, Rta Kapur, Singh, Martand, *Saris of India: Tradition and Beyond*, Roli Books, 2010.

Dwivedi Shalini, Holkar, Shalini Devi, *Almond Eyes: Lotus Feet,* Collins, 2007.

Eames, Charles and Ray, The India Report, National Institute of Design, 1958, http://nid.edu/Userfiles/Eames___India_Report.pdf

Jain, Jyotindra, *Indian Popular Culture: The Conquest of the World as Picture*, NGMA, 2004.

Jain, Jyotindra, *Utensils: An Introduction to the Utensils Museum Ahmedabad*, Surendra C. Patel for Vechaar Foundation, 1984.

Kothari, K.S., *Indian Folk Musical Instruments*, Sangeet Natak Akademi, 1968.

May, Gordon G., *Royal Enfield: The Legend Rides On*, Celebrating 50 Years in India, Royal Enfield/Eicher Motors, 2005.

Cort, Louise Allison, and Mishra, Purna Chandra, *Temple Potters of Puri*, Louise Allison Cort, Mapin Publishing, 2012.

Mukharji, T.N., Art-manufactures of India, Calcutta Government Printing, 1888.

Najar, Nida, 'An Icon of Indian Roads is Set out to Pasture', *New York Times*, June 2014, https://www.nytimes.com/2014/06/27/world/asia/an-icon-of-indian-roads-is-setout-to-pasture.html.

Pathak, Anamika and National Museum, *Pashmina*, Roli Books, 2004.

Ray, Acharya Prafulla Chandra, *History of Chemistry in Ancient and Medieval India: Incorporating the History of Hindu Chemistry*, Indian Chemical Society, 1956.

Rizvi, Janet, and Ahmed, Monisha, *Pashmina: The Kashmir Shawl and Beyond*, The Marg Foundation, 2009.

Sen, A.K., 'The Pattern of British Enterprise in India 1815–1914: A Causal Analysis', in Baljit Singh and V.B. Singh, *Social and Economic Change, Essays in Honour of Prof. D.P. Mukherji*, Allied Publishers Private Limited, 1966, pp. 409–427.

Sen, Amartya, *The Argumentative Indian: Writings on Indian History, Culture and Identity*, Penguin UK, 2005.

Shah, Haku, 'Form and Many Forms of Mother Clay: Contemporary Indian Pottery and Terracotta', Exhibition and Catalogue, 1985.

Singh, Vikram, 'Road Ends for India's Ambassador, *New York Times*, June 2014, https://www.nytimes.com/video/world/asia/100000002953621/road-ends-for-indias-ambassador.html?mcubz=0.

Swarup, Sushma, *Costumes and Textiles of Awadh: From the Era of Nawabs to Modern Times*, Roli Books, 2012.

Tata Nano: The People's Car, 2009

Tiwari, S.P., *Nupura: The Anklet in Indian Literature and Art*, Agam Kala Prakashan, 2007.

www.rareindianfacts.org

CREDITS

Photographer: Shivani Gupta
Editors: Radhika Jha, Priya Kapoor, Aditi Chopra
Assistant Photographer: Jagan Khursule
Designologist: Aradhana Seth
Researchers: Kaveri Nandan, Puja Vaish
Contributing images: Munir Kabani, Tarun Sehdev, Anisha Saigal
Page 29, Bajaj Chetak © Eye Ubiquitous/Dinodia
Design: Sneha Pamneja
Project Coordinator: Anisha Saigal
Pre-press: Jyoti Dey
Layout: Naresh L. Mondal
Production: Yuvraj Singh